PEN DRAWING

AND PEN DRAUGHTSMEN

PEN DRAWING AND PEN DRAUGHTSMEN

THEIR WORK AND THEIR METHODS.
A STUDY OF THE ART
WITH TECHNICAL SUGGESTIONS.

JOSEPH PENNELL

HART PUBLISHING COMPANY, INC.   NEW YORK CITY

ISBN NO. 08055-1127-X (PAPERBACK 08055-0218-1)

MANUFACTURED IN THE UNITED STATES OF AMERICA

JOSEPH PENNELL

Throughout his forty-four year career as illustrator, etcher, and lithographer, Joseph Pennell sought to communicate his ideas and opinions on the arts he practiced. This gifted artist and craftsman has left volumes, vital with his theories, to inspire generations of art students and to enlighten the public.

Born in 1857, Pennell received his training in Philadelphia and London. The American public was first introduced to his illustrations in 1882, when the Century Company published "A Ramble in Old Philadelphia." The text, written by Pennell's future wife, was accompanied by eight of Pennell's etchings of historical buildings.

Pennell and his bride, matched by the Century Company as author and artist, moved to London where they continued publishing pieces on their European excursions. Pennell also began illustrating the works of well-known authors of the day.

A prodigious artist, Pennell produced an enormous body of work— 900 etchings, 621 lithographs, countless drawings, watercolors, and illustrated volumes, a biography of James MacNeill Whistler, and a series of eight books on the practice of art. Committed to sharing the knowledge and skill acquired over a lifetime, Pennell spent his last years at the Art Students League in New York, teaching and encouraging a new generation of artists.

Though he never studied under him, the influence of Whistler's philosophy is easily detected in Pennell's drawings. In Whistler's singular concern for the surface of a subject, Pennell found the answer to a basic complexity inherent in illustration—the problem of making an interesting drawing of that which may hold no interest to the artist. The central focus for Pennell's philosophy was his belief in the pictorial unimportance of a subject as compared to the artistry and workmanship employed in the execution of the drawing itself.

Pennell envisioned the artist's role as that of a reporter, recording what men did and made. He was driven by a passion for the practical—for things that worked. He had no patience or interest in listening to an inner muse, but was drawn to any object in his environment that demanded workmanship. What fascinated Pennell were the products of man's hands—buildings, cisterns, engines, machines.

Obsessed with the objects that characterized his time, Pennell chose his subject matter, his loyalties, and the men he admired by the yardstick of workmanship. He was one of the first to record the physical realities of modern industrial life, in a time when other artists were involved in creating charming little scenes of faraway places.

Pennell's work celebrated the last phase of the Industrial Revolution. He saw dignity and grandiose beauty in the objects and environment created during an era that sacrificed individuality to corporate enterprise.

At the conclusion of his career as an illustrator, Pennell became completely absorbed in the subject matter of his independent art—what he called the "wonder of work." He traveled incessantly, observing men at work, noting man's triumphs of materials, recording the smoke and smell and noise of an industrial world.

Many critics contend that the least of Pennell's accomplishments are the skillful, charming drawings of his younger years when his subject merely provided him with an opportunity for illustration. Pennell's real power as an artist is contained in his later etchings and lithographs which depict his profound belief in the grandeur of corporate labor concentrated in achieving practical human goals.

Pennell left us a legacy of great value. His drawings, etchings, and lithographs preserve the architecture and environment of many European cities as they appeared in the late 19th century, and some of the now vanished realities of American life. Pennell's volumes on the practice of art, still vibrant with his concepts, remain a repository of insight into illustration, etching, and lithography.

                                                    PAM POLLACK

PEN DRAWING

AND PEN DRAUGHTSMEN

PREFACE

POPULAR illustration is the product of the nineteenth century. It has never been treated seriously, and to-day it covers such a wide field and is so many-sided that it is impossible to discuss more than one of its phases at a time. The best illustrators are as conscientious in their profession as the best painters or sculptors. But with the enormous growth of, and demand for, illustration, draughtsmen have appeared who care nothing at all for their art, whose only desire apparently is to produce more than any one else, and who threaten, owing to the cheapness and rapidity with which they work and the avidity with which certain publishers seize upon the results, to drag illustration down to their own low level. I have endeavoured to show what a high standard the best illustration reaches, and to give, for purposes of study, the most notable examples from all over the world.

I am afraid my book may not appeal very strongly to the book-lover, since in it I have transgressed many of the established laws of book-making, and thought more of facing the text with the appropriate illustration than of the size and shape of the page. In some cases the actual appearance of the drawing as book decoration is very unpleasant to me. But it was a case of sacrificing either practical examples for study, or else here and there the decoration of a page. If the book is to have any value, it must be of use to the student; therefore, in certain places I have not kept to traditional forms. I object as much as any one to the meaningless and senseless dotting of pictures over the margin and their eccentric arrangement on the page, and I think it will be realised that necessity, and not eccentricity, has occasioned any placing of the cuts in other than the true decorative form.

It is also because the book is intended primarily for the student that I publish much work that has been seen before, gathered from every available source and put together, I hope it will be found, not in a haphazard manner, but as carefully as I could. Many artists have been consulted in the selection; to many others it will probably be a surprise to see their drawings here; I think there are very few whom, from ignorance of their work, I have omitted. I have not included examples of very original men like Manet and Jean Béraud, for, though I admire their work as the supreme expression of individuality and originality, it is only of value from the man who produces it, and the copy by the student is worse than worthless. And for the same reason examples of many well-known comic draughtsmen will not be found; their reputation is based on their wit and humour which cannot be imitated, while the student can learn nothing from their technique. I trust the critic may not be obliged to point out that I have forgotten any well-known pen draughtsmen or important pen drawings published during the last half-century, within which time pen drawing has taken rank as a separate art. If I have unwittingly overlooked any one, I shall be only too glad, if I am allowed the chance, to insert or describe his work on a future occasion. The spelling of some of the names of lesser known artists may be questioned, while there is at least one man whose nationality may be wrongly given. But when artists themselves spell their names in three or four fashions, I cannot be expected to know which is right; I have tried to use the most common form. And when they are continually changing their nationality, one cannot tell to what country they really belong.

Where old reproductions have been used it has not been for cheapness, but because these reproductions were the best made at the time the drawings were published, and because if I had commissioned—and Messrs. Macmillan were willing to order—drawings from artists of established reputation, it is extremely doubtful, even for this purpose, if they would have surpassed the best work they had already done, and my object has been to show their best work. While in the making of the book I have had the interest and enthusiasm, generosity and encouragement of the leading publishers with very few exceptions, these few to my great surprise have come altogether from France, and I have no hesitation in saying that they have prevented my including either any work of certain artists or that which I specially desired.

Many critics and literary men have allowed themselves to be carried away in praise of drawings which artists cannot respect, and have even devoted volumes to the work of men and women whose names are not in the following pages. But my book is technical, and unless a drawing possesses technique I care not a jot or a tittle for its intellectual, social, or spiritual qualities. Without technical merit such work is useless for study. I have made no endeavour to estimate the value of the drawing of the artists represented, nor to claim for them any place among the immortals. I believe much of the work will live and will be known as long as there is any real love for art. But since all the greatest men here represented, with one or two exceptions, are living and working to-day, it is impossible to form any estimate of the place they will occupy in the future, nor is it my business to do so.

In the preparation of the book, instead of having, as in most cases, authorities to consult and acknowledgment to make for information gained from them, I can only say that there are no authorities on my subject, this indeed being one of my reasons for writing. No works of importance, so far as I have been able to discover, have been written upon pen drawing since the introduction of process which has made it into a separate and distinct art. However, I have deep acknowledgments to make to artists,—the real but usually unconsulted and ignored authorities,—to publishers, and, above all, to my wife.

This book, which is the outcome of Mr. Richmond Seeley's offer to publish a small handbook on pen drawing, would never have appeared in its present form, had not Mrs. Pennell devoted much time to the writing from my dictation of the text. She has managed all the correspondence in connection with it, and relieved me of the drudgery of the work. Without her aid and encouragement, the almost insurmountable difficulties, altogether unforeseen but encountered at every step, could not have been overcome.

I must next thank Messrs. Macmillan, especially Mr. Frederick Macmillan, for their generosity in allowing the illustrations to be so complete, for their permission to use or reproduce drawings which have appeared in their publications, and for their willingness to reject process block after process block, the most imperfect of which perhaps not half a dozen people in the world would have criticised.

The Century Company, my friends and patrons—for publishers to-day are the greatest art patrons who ever lived,—have freely lent me all the drawings I wanted from their unrivalled collection. In this matter I am particularly indebted to Mr. Charles F. Chichester, the assistant treasurer, and Messrs. A. W. Drake and W. Lewis Fraser, the art editors.

Mr. David Douglas of Edinburgh has lent me the plate by Amand-Durand after Mr. George Reid. Messrs. George Routledge and Sons have also contributed the blocks after Randolph Caldecott engraved by Mr. Edmund Evans. Messrs. Harper have given me permission to use the two drawings by Messrs. Abbey and Parsons from She Stoops to Conquer ; *and Mr. Charles Parsons, the late head of their Art Department, was good enough to select drawings and have electros under his supervision made from them in New York. Messrs. Carrère and Hastings undertook the printing of an edition of Blum's drawing from their book on the Ponce de Leon Hotel; while Messrs. Cassell, Charles Scribner's Sons of New York, Bradbury, Agnew and Co., and R. Seeley and Co., have furnished me with editions and plates and blocks from their different publications. As to the great mass of French, German, Italian, and Spanish work, with the exception of original drawings, it was obtained through the Electrotype Agency, the proprietor of which, Mr. D. T. Nops, has on several occasions gone to much trouble in obtaining certain electros, as well as in other matters.*

But after all there would be no illustrated publications were it not for artists and engravers, and from them I have received directly more sympathy and substantial assistance than I ever could have expected. It is useless to specify the many interesting letters I have received from all quarters of the world. But when in several cases these letters have been accompanied by original drawings as freely given as they have been gratefully accepted, I hardly know how duly to acknowledge the kindness. On commissioning Martin Rico to make a drawing, he gave me with it another quite as important—the one which begins the chapter on his work—simply, as he put it, as a petit souvenir. *Casanova, refusing to make a drawing at any price, sent instead what he called a little sketch; it appears as a full-page photogravure. I must also specially acknowledge my indebtedness to Messrs. Alfred Parsons, E. A. Abbey, Wirgman, W. L. Wyllie, George Reid, David Murray, Mackmurdo and Horne, Harry Furniss, Linley Sambourne, and the artists of* Pick-Me-Up; *while I must at least refer to the kindly aid and interest of Adolf Menzel, Vierge, Dantan, Mme. Lemaire, Messrs. W. M. Rossetti, Howard Pyle, Charles Keene, and J. G. Legge, the latter having attended to many difficult business details for me in Paris. But the list is endless. I have already tried to thank each individually; I am glad to be able to again thank all collectively.*

Messrs. Dalziel with the greatest possible generosity—a generosity which can only be appreciated when I say that these drawings were lent solely for the purpose of endeavouring to surpass their own woodcuts, in which I have succeeded —furnished me with the original drawings by Sir Frederick Leighton, Messrs. F. M. Brown and Poynter, which were published in their Bible Gallery. *Messrs. Dalziel and Swain have not only given me much invaluable information about the greatest period of English illustration with which they were so intimately associated, but Mr. Swain has also furnished me with the photographic negative from which the Sandys plate was made. As to the photo-engravers who have been particularly successful in the reproduction of drawings, I have sought to give them due credit where their work appears.*

I have not space to mention all the collectors I have bothered, all the collections I have waded through, but I must at least allow myself the pleasure of again thanking Mr. J. P. Heseltine for lending me the drawing by Frederick Walker, Mr. Edmund Gosse for his book plate by Mr. Abbey, and Mr. Hall for the drawing by the same artist from She Stoops to Conquer. *The authorities of the British and South Kensington Museums will probably remember me as one who has given them an immense amount of muscular exercise in the mere carting of bound magazines; the fact that they not only never rebelled, save on one occasion in the British Museum, but were willing to aid me by other than physical means, calls for my very best thanks.*

I must also explain that when I say that American printing is the best, I refer especially to magazine work—that is the rapid printing of large editions. But this would not be true in speaking of the printing of a book like this. Messrs. Clark have taken the greatest possible pains with it, and have been completely successful. I do not believe it could have been better printed anywhere.

WESTMINSTER, *August* 1889.

PEN DRAWING
AND PEN DRAUGHTSMEN

CONTENTS

CONTENTS

PEN DRAWING
AND PEN DRAUGHTSMEN

LIST OF ILLUSTRATIONS

Note.—Many of the plates and blocks being unsigned, I am unfortunately unable in certain cases to give the engravers who reproduced them credit for their work. There are also a few illustrations to which the date of publication is not appended. This is due to the fact that either original drawings were sent me by artists or publishers without date or title, or else examples were selected from unsigned and undated collections of proofs.

PEN DRAWING & PEN DRAUGHTSMEN

INTRODUCTION

THERE are three reasons why I wish to write of pen drawing at the present time. The first is because I believe that, just as none but the physician is allowed to speak with authority on medicine, none but the scientist on science, so only the man who has made and carefully studied pen drawings should have the right to speak authoritatively of them. Only the writing on art by one who has technical knowledge of it is of practical value, and I think this explains why it is, that of the many books on art written of late years, so few are of real use to the artist. Such volumes as Lalanne's *Treatise on Etching*, Mr. Hamerton's *Etching and Etchers*, and some parts of Ruskin's *Elements of Drawing*, are indeed the exceptions.

This leads me to my second reason for writing : the very unsatisfactory manner in which pen drawing has hitherto been treated. The principal critics of the day hold their own estimation of contemporary and earlier art in all its many branches to be the only right one, and abuse every other as vitally at fault ; while it is the tendency of many modern writers to so enlarge upon the divine mission, the intellectual value, the historical importance of art in the past, as to belittle contemporary art, and to altogether ignore technique, which is as great to-day as in any former time. Without the nearest possible individual approach to technical perfection, according to the standard of the age in which it is produced, art work cannot be of value as a whole, although in parts it may be instructive.

If often this belittling of contemporary art is to be expected, it is unwarranted when extended to pen drawing, which, as a distinct art, belongs only to the last few years. This fact has been so completely overlooked that in treatises accepted as authorities, pen drawing in its modern development has not received the attention it deserves. This is true even of Mr. Hamerton's chapter on the subject, though it must be remembered that *The Graphic Arts* was published in 1882, before pen drawing had developed to any extent in England; and, knowing how careful and painstaking Mr. Hamerton is in all his work, I think it probable that this chapter was written at a much earlier date. Looking in *The Graphic Arts*, I find that not one of the pen drawings is reproduced by any intaglio process of photo-engraving, and it is the development of photo-engraving, side by side with pen drawing, that has brought the latter to its present perfection.

Of course the pen drawings or sketches of Albert Dürer, of Da Vinci and Raphael, of Michael Angelo and Titian, in fact of every old master, and above all of Rembrandt, are unquestionably instructive and interesting and curious. Of the drawings of several of these men I shall speak further on. As a rule, however, they are but memoranda, the adjuncts of another art. To-day pen drawing is not only an art in itself, but one which, as well as painting in oils, requires its own technical perfection. It may be objected that the old masters often made elaborate pen drawings. So they did; just as Rossetti elaborated with his pen or pencil until one wishes he had put the same time and infinite amount of work that went to his illustrations of Tennyson, and copies of his pictures, for example, into his beautiful pastels. True, in the end he succeeded in getting what he wanted, but he was no technician; like the old masters, he did not in the modern sense know how to make a pen drawing. I should except some of his slight early sketches, and notably a fine head of his mother.

With a certain class of writers on art I am not here concerned, since to them eloquent writing is of more importance than honest criticism, and their ignorance of the technique of any art is only equalled by their ability to write on it. There have been men, however, who have sought to treat pen and ink drawing technically, and the third reason for my writing is that some of these writers, who call themselves pen draughtsmen, have evidently the very smallest knowledge of their subject. One such manual states on cover and title-page that pen and ink drawing is commonly called etching, showing at once to what manner of audience it is addressed, viz. people who draw with pen and ink on antimacassars and call it etching, and who are continually asking what is the difference between a pen drawing and an etching anyway.[1] If Mr. Hamerton and Mr. Ruskin have not been able to show this elementary difference, it would be not only presumptuous, but a great waste of paper on my part to quote their words. However, for the benefit of such people, to whom it probably will be information, I may say that pen drawing is, was, and ever shall be, drawing with a pen, and nothing else. As to etching, it is a method of engraving on a metal plate with which I am not here concerned.

Neither do I propose to make this a treatise on drawing. For one must not only know something of art, but all that one can find out for one's self about drawing, before good work can be done with the pen. Strange as it may seem to the crowds who are actually flooding the world with pen drawings, the same qualities go to make a good pen drawing which Mr. Hamerton rightly says are indispensable to the production of a good etching. The only advantage is, that instead of having a treacherous material to work with, you have the simplest possible. This being so, only proves the great difficulty of really drawing well with the pen.

When one sees pen and ink copies of woodcuts, of oil paintings, of anything and everything, all worked out with an awful and reverent, but utterly misplaced and wasted fidelity, one best realises that pen drawing, like etching, is one of the most facile, least understood, and most abused of the arts.

I do not believe with one of the few men who have already written of pen drawing that he or any one else can, in a book, "teach drawing in Indian ink, upon principles so easy and progressive that

[1] The Master of the Architectural School of the Royal Academy also falls into this careless mistake. On page 47, paragraph 143, of his *Architectural Drawing*, writing of pen drawings, he illustrates his matter by reference to what he calls a perspective *etched* in brown ink. Other architects are continually talking of a drawing being etched when they mean it is drawn in pen and ink.

individuals may attain this pleasing amusement without the aid of a master"; or indeed, unless the student has great ability, with his aid. But I am not without hope that the pen drawings published here will show many, who are pleased to call themselves pen draughtsmen, that they are without the faintest idea of the aims, objects, and limitations of the art; as well as bring to the notice of amateurs, collectors, critics and print-sellers, a healthy, vigorous, flourishing art which is being developed and improved in all its branches, and owes nothing whatever to their fostering care or encouragement.

For examples, I have selected the best work, so far as I have been able to find it, of all schools, and not merely of one narrow French, English, Italian, German, Spanish, or American method, the merits or shortcomings of which one would be unable to point out without using this comparative plan.

Mr. Hamerton calls pen drawing a "simple process," and some people may unwisely suppose that a simple process implies an easy and trifling form of art. To the incipient artist encouraged by the financial success of pen drawing hacks, I would only say: unless you feel that pen drawing is something to be reverenced, something to be studied, something to be loved, something to be wondered at, that you are the motive power behind the pen, and that you must put all your individuality and character into your work, you will never become a pen draughtsman. And you should be prouder to illustrate the greatest magazines of the world, thus appealing to millions of readers, than to have your drawings buried in the portfolios of a few hundred collectors. For I believe that, in these days, artists, who show their work to the people through the press, are doing as did the masters of other days, who spoke to the people through the church.

PEN DRAWING IN THE PAST

PEN DRAWING IN THE PAST

OF pen drawing in the past I shall say but little, for the simple reason that there is little to be said. No artist would study the old masters, with a very few exceptions, notably among the old Dutchmen, for the technical qualities of pen drawing. As painters now look to Titian and Velasquez, Rembrandt and Franz Hals, so men in future times will look back to some of the pen draughtsmen of to-day as not only the early, but the great masters of the art. It is not necessary to do more than to point out the scope and aim of pen drawing as it existed among the great artists of other days, in order to emphasise its far wider scope and higher aims among the men of the present. A knowledge of its immaturity in the past helps one to the appreciation of its development in our own time.

It must be understood, however, that if the pen drawing of the old masters was undeveloped in comparison with the work of to-day, it was simply because with them there was no call for it as an art apart. It was quite perfect for the purpose they wished it to serve. Since in engravings on wood and steel all the pen quality of a drawing is lost, when they wanted to reproduce their work autographically, they etched. What Mr. Hamerton says generally of pen drawings, is really applicable only to theirs: they were " sketches of projects and intentions." They are to be studied, of course, for their composition and arrangement, suggestion of light and shade, and rendering of the figure, of which I have no intention to speak, since in these matters pen drawing is subject to the same laws as any other art; but for pure technique these pen memoranda, as a rule, have little to teach the modern draughtsman.

That the old masters made great use of the pen is well enough known. One cannot go to any of the galleries of the world without seeing many of their pen drawings, which are interesting in their relation to the pictures of which they were the germs, and as records of strong impressions and ideas vigorously and simply put down. And here let me insist again that, while one may make notes and sketches as they did, and study their marvellous facility and vigour in so sketching, such sketches are not, as many modern art critics and artists consider them, pen drawings. This is proved at once by the very different methods used by these same masters in their etchings, to which the pen drawings of to-day are equivalent. But their pen sketches, or rather memoranda, really were for them very much what instantaneous photographs are for the modern artist— suggestions and notes of action and movement. By all means these old sketches should be studied. But it is the veriest affectation nowadays to imitate them.

If the artists of to-day were not possessed of such external aids as photography, they would probably excel all old masters in sketching—always excepting Rembrandt, though Whistler in his etchings of architecture is quite the equal of Rembrandt. The modern artist has many aids and adjuncts which the old men knew nothing about, and which make the work of to-day much more true and accurate and scientific than that of any other time. But because of his dependence on these aids, the modern artist has lost much of the old facility in sketching. What I say applies even to colour. And if a man with the gifts of Titian were to come to-day, he would surpass Titian himself, just as Corot surpasses all the old landscapists.

Michael Angelo, Da Vinci, and Raphael often made the first sketches for their pictures with pen and ink: sketches full of character, which have lately been made better known by Braun's autotypes and numberless photographs. Botticelli's delicate and refined illustrations for the *Divina Commedia*, though drawn in with sympathetic silver point, were gone over with pen and ink.

Landscapes by Titian, with little villages or houses in the middle distance, have a delightful suggestion of picturesqueness; but it is curious to compare these with modern pen and ink landscapes by Rico or Vierge, for example. Titian's, the honest critic must admit, suffer when comparison of their technical points is made. A drawing of a Turk by Giovanni Bellini in the British Museum can, for beauty of modelling with a pen and delicacy of handling combined with simplicity, be advantageously studied by the pen draughtsmen of to-day. It shows what the old men might have done with a pen.

There are pen studies of horses and carriages by Velasquez, very simply and strongly suggested. But it is unnecessary to go through the list of all the masters whose drawings have been preserved. It is endless, and, differing as the drawings do in character, they are nearly all alike in being mere notes or records of facts; or if, as rarely happens, carried out, they are, save in few more than the cases I have mentioned, valueless for study of technique. There are ideas enough to be learned from them, and sometimes the best and strongest work of the artist is to be found in his pen drawings.

The pen draughtsman will study to best advantage such old work as Holbein's *Dance of Death*, and beautiful designs for metal work, many of the originals of which may be found in the British Museum; Albert Dürer's and Israel von Meckenen's engravings; Rembrandt's etchings; the lovely Renaissance decorative head and tail pieces. Dürer, having no perfect process by which to reproduce his work, wisely put little delicacy of line into his wonderful drawings for the wood-cutter, and delicacy is all that is lacking to make them in technique equal to the drawings of to-day. That he could draw delicately is shown by his etchings, every one of which is worthy of reverent study. That he did not, only proves that he understood the limitations of wood-cutting. This want, however, added to a certain archaic decorative feeling that pervades all his engraved work, makes it affectation for an artist to-day to model his style on that of Dürer.

But, on the other hand, nothing could be nearer perfection for an artist of a northern country to study than Rembrandt's drawings and etchings of out-of-door subjects, especially his little views of towns. Even Mr. Ruskin gives this advice in his *Elements of Drawing*. Rembrandt's etchings have so many of the same qualities as pen drawings that, I feel certain, had he lived in our age, he would not have etched so much, but would have made innumerable pen drawings, for the same reason the best pen draughtsman of to-day, who could etch if he chose, once gave me. Why, when he could have his drawings reproduced perfectly, should he use a nasty, dirty process, which is successful more by good luck than good management? You can see by reproductions in the *Gazette des Beaux-Arts* how well Rembrandt's simpler etchings, as well as Vandyke's, are rendered by process blocks from clean wiped prints. Many of Rembrandt's etchings come very well without any wiping.[1] Collectors now appreciate old etchings for their rarity, but when they were made, they were appreciated because of their perfect reproduction of the master's work. There were then no fancy prices attached to Rembrandt's etchings, or, in his time, to Méryon's either for that matter. They were sold for a few pence, as are our best illustrated magazines.

There is a little of the modern feeling and go in some of Tiepolo's drawings. Claude's landscape sketching in pen and ink is also marked by more of the modern spirit. Mr. Hamerton, indeed, thinks that with him modern pen work began. Both these artists used washes of bistre or sepia in their pen drawings. But to this I see no reason to make objection. I am no purist in art, and therefore no advocate for "pure pen drawing." I think it more important to give a desired effect, no matter how, than to limit the means by which it is to be obtained.

The development from Claude and Tiepolo, through Paul Huet and others, onwards to our time, could be easily traced. Doubtless many pages could be filled were I to follow this growth in detail, and the average art critic would have ample opportunity to discover my omissions and praise my discoveries. But I do not think it worth while, since it is in its maturity, rather than in its making, that pen drawing is most interesting. And besides, as I have said, the introduction of photo-engraving had so much to do with its development that there seems to be but one step from the old "sketches of projects and intentions" to the modern comparatively perfect work.

The history of the development of pen drawing and the history

[1] For reproductions of Rembrandt's etchings by process, see *Les Artistes Célèbres; Rembrandt*, par Emile Michel, Paris; *Librairie de L'Art*, 1886; and *Daheim*, Leipzic, Sept. 1888, *seq.*

of the development of photo-engraving are two distinct subjects, neither of which do I propose to treat. Mr. H. Trueman Wood in his *Modern Methods of Illustrating Books* devotes a chapter to mechanical processes, in which he gives the bare dates and facts about photo-engraving. I think it more than likely that the processes he mentions were used in France and America before they were ever attempted in this country, though Mr. Fraser of the *Century* says the first really successful process was Woodbury's in England. However, the first successful reproductions which appeared in any English magazine, I have found in *Once a Week*, and they were taken from French periodicals.

There are, on the other hand, innumerable histories and biographies of the great and lesser masters of all times from Giotto to the man who died yesterday, all of whom have helped to develop pen drawing. But until about the year 1880 pen drawing did not begin to flourish as an art in itself. Before this no artist, except as an experiment, would have his work reproduced by these, then, only partially developed processes. The drawings of the old masters, when reproduced at all, were drawn on wood and then cut all to pieces, and this method was continued until a very few years ago, when photography was made use of to transfer the image of natural objects on to the wood. Thence it was only a step to photograph the pen or other drawing on to the block, the original work remaining untouched. The last step of all is the photographing of the pen or other drawing—with pen drawings alone I am of course here concerned—on to a sensitised block, gelatine film or zinc plate, or other substance, from which a mechanical or process engraving is made. It is this development of process which has made pen drawing into a distinct art, equal in importance to etching.

Throughout this volume I use the word process to express the reproduction of a drawing. It is the word used by artists, and therefore the right one.

PEN DRAWING IN THE PAST

ILLUSTRATIONS

TITIAN

I SHOW this drawing by Titian, and with it a little sketch in Holland by Maxime Lalanne, for the purpose of comparison. I am quite aware that it will be thought absurd on my part to compare the study for a great picture, which this may have been,—I confess I do not know for what picture it was a study, if indeed it was ever used, for I cannot recall any of Titian's pictures in which the composition recurs,—with an apparently slight and trivial drawing by Lalanne. I know it will at once be said that the hand of a greater man and a larger and broader mind is shown in a pen drawing which, like Titian's, can give a rocky foreground with a great tree, a middle distance with a town and woods, a lake stretching away to a mountainous horizon, and above all, a fine cloud effect. I would be the first to admit this, if the drawing by Titian expressed, with the same simplicity and meaning of line, a result as artistic as that of the drawing by Lalanne. But this is certainly not the case.

Before analysing Titian's drawing, I must do that which will seem gratuitous. I must make an apology for it by saying that I do not believe Titian ever intended it to be shown. And because Titian was one of the greatest, if not the greatest Italian painter who ever lived, there is absolutely no reason why we should bow down and worship everything that came from his hand. Though the composition is suggestive and may have been of great value to the artist, the actual lines are useless for study. They are careless and trivial from one end of the drawing to the other. To come down to details, the idea of the tree trunk which comes out towards us is very well given, although there is in it absolutely no feeling for line. But it grows out of a meaningless blot at the bottom and disappears at the top in meaningless scrawls which common sense tells us are meant for foliage. Compare it for a moment with the young tree by Lalanne;[1] note how gracefully the growth of the tree is indicated, and the way in which Lalanne shows the direction of the prevalent wind in Holland, which causes the tree to bend and its branches to grow on the side away from it. Then in Titian's drawing it is impossible to tell where the rocky foreground ends and the water of the lake begins, even though the lake lies far below. Everything is obscure. In Lalanne's this is shown in the clearest manner with about one-third the number of lines Titian has used. In the Titian there are blots in the water, and you cannot make out the construc-

tion of the boat. In the Lalanne this is plain enough; you can even see the different colours in which his boat is painted. Look at the careful and yet slight indication of the roadway leading back to the towered gate. But can any one tell me what the cross-hatched, scrawled-in hill on the right of Titian's is composed of? Titian's middle distance of a town, woods, and a house under the trees on the opposite side of the lake have the handling of a small child, while the perspective is all out. In Lalanne's, note how every line has a purpose, how beautifully the shadows are given on the houses, how the little

[1] La Porte Saint-Antoine, Amsterdam. *La Hollande à Vol d'Oiseau*, Henry Havard, Decaux, and Quantin, Paris.

blots all have a meaning, while Titian's are due to pure carelessness. There is quite as much suggestion in Lalanne's pure white paper sky, as in Titian's laboured clouds. I know that any critic can see these things. But the point I wish to emphasise is that students are bidden, and do study drawings like this of Titian's; because he was a great master of painting, he is supposed to be a great master of everything; but Lalanne, who was an equally great master as a pen draughtsman, is ignored because he is a modern and rarely painted. And I want to insist in the strongest manner that this, and all other drawings of Titian's I have ever seen—and I have gone through almost all the great galleries,—are simply of no value whatever for the study of technique. I repeat what I have already said that neither pen drawing nor landscape painting was then developed, or had even become an independent and separate art of any great importance. I do not for a moment assert that Titian could not have made a fine pen drawing. I only say that, judging from his drawings which we possess, he did not.

NOTE.—For other Lalannes, see Illustrations to Chapter on French Pen Drawing.

SOME COMPARATIVE HEADS:
OLD AND NEW

IN showing these heads I have thought it best to compare the old work with the new, even though I am thus grouping together two or three different countries, in order to explain more easily the difference between ancient and modern methods.

Commencing with Dürer; we all know what he could do with a pen from his designs and decorations, so refined as to be models for use to-day, and from his woodcuts, for whether he drew these with a pen, pencil, or brush is of very little importance since the results resemble pen drawings on the block. But when we come upon a drawing like this, of which he must have been proud or he would never have signed it, we find at once, exquisite though

the drawing is and fine as is every line in it, that Dürer had not a knowledge of the wealth and depth of colour which can be obtained with a pen. By comparing it with the drawing by Rossetti this becomes apparent, even though the Rossetti has lost very much in the woodcut. The lines in the Dürer are

of course far finer than those in the Rossetti, but the latter suggests far more colour and is much more freely handled than the earlier drawing of Dürer. Neither of these drawings was intended for reproduction, and the Dürer no more resembles his etchings than the Rossetti resembles his designs which were put on the block.

That a man like Vandyke, for example, could draw with a pen is shown most conclusively by the accompanying head of a child, though, of course, in his day such a drawing could never have been reproduced; but to-day it could be, as indeed it has been perfectly. Even the chalk work in it comes admirably. However, the head of Mme. Madrazo by Galice, though not to be compared with it in knowledge of form or in beauty of line, in some ways shows plainly the advances we have made technically. While all of Vandyke's shadows are made, or at any rate have been reproduced in nearly pure black, Galice's, being drawn with a fine pen, give variety to the whole, and allow him to concentrate his blacks where he wants. Vandyke has scattered his blacks all over. Nevertheless his drawing is but another proof that the old men could have drawn with a pen had there been any necessity for it.

I have had a process made from Vandyke's etching of the head of Snyders and it is upon his etchings that Vandyke's reputation as a black-and-white man rests. I have placed with it two heads by Louis Desmoulins from *La Vie Moderne*, which I think any one must admit are quite equal to Vandyke's work, and yet utterly different.

The smaller drawing is as full of character and the modelling as well given as in the Vandyke; in the larger one the feeling of flesh is far more completely carried out than in the Vandyke, while the hair, moustache, and imperial, somewhat similar in both, are vastly better rendered by Desmoulins. Here is a man who, I venture to say, is almost unknown, and yet in black and white he has surpassed Vandyke with his world-wide reputation. However, Vandyke has had but a handful of followers; Desmoulins, whether the fact is known to newspaper

editors or not, is the man who commenced the drawing of portraits in pen and ink for illustrated journalism. Vandyke gave to a few of his friends a most interesting gallery of his contemporaries; Desmoulins has given the whole world a most artistic rendering of many great and little Frenchmen, and has influenced a vast army of pen draughtsmen of whom he still remains the master.

These drawings also demonstrate another fact: we moderns have advanced very little, if at all, in merely getting a likeness. But we have made great strides in technical execution in the drawing of portraits. If any one

will dispassionately compare the manner in which Vandyke has dotted and stippled the light side of the face of Snyders, and lined the shadows without reference to the modelling, with the very simple yet suggestive line of Desmoulins, he will find that Desmoulins has carried his subject further and rendered the head more completely with an expenditure of probably half the time and labour. The actual time and labour given to a drawing is of course of no importance. But if one can show a good result produced simply, it cannot but be an advantage.

As I have said elsewhere I should like to give the beautiful Bellini—the drawing of a Turk—which is in the British Museum. But the delicate lines are so faded it would have been impossible to render them adequately. It has more of the spirit of a modern pen drawing than any old pen work I have seen.

REMBRANDT

REMBRANDT, great in every way, shows his knowledge of the limitation of every art by his admirable and right work in it.   The etching of the old man's head here given is a perfect study for a pen sketch.   It is as free as it can be, and yet every line is put in carefully.   The most positive proof that Rembrandt would have been a pen draughtsman had he lived to-day is the fact that this head reproduces charmingly by process.   Compare it with the head of the master in the Unfaithful Servant, the full-page pen drawing, and note that though every line in the latter is put down with a purpose, and there is in it none of the wild scrawling so visible in Titian, it is without the delicacy and refinement shown in the two etchings.   It is only a note to be used in a picture or an etching, and I am sure is not a work upon which Rembrandt would have wished to base his reputation.

As I have said of other men, Rembrandt knew perfectly the limitations of pen drawing in his day and he respected them.   When he wanted the quality which now is to be had in pen drawing, he etched, and in his simple etchings, which are not dependent on dry point, he obtained this quality, though of course they possessed a certain softness which no process has yet been able to give. No man among the ancients is greater than Rembrandt as an etcher, but Whistler in his etchings of Old London is even greater than Rembrandt. Therefore, if you wish a simple style good for all times, you will find it in many of these landscape and figure subjects of Rembrandt's.   But for work of to-day —and Rembrandt gave the things that were about him—the student would learn more from the work of Whistler.

SPANISH AND ITALIAN WORK

PEN DRAWING OF TO-DAY

SPANISH AND ITALIAN WORK

PEN drawing as an art in itself belongs to the nineteenth century, especially to the last quarter. Mr. Hamerton, who in his *Graphic Arts* gives a brief sketch of its history, says: "Fortuny, the Spanish painter, introduced a new kind of pen drawing which has been followed by Casanova and others of the same school, and which has had some influence outside of it, as well as upon the practice of etching."

But when he wrote, though but six years ago, the real significance of this new kind of pen drawing had not been brought to the notice of even so keen an observer. For the truth is, in Fortuny's day pen drawing was revolutionised; he, Madrazo, Rico and Vierge in Spain, Menzel and Dietz in Germany, Lalanne and De Neuville in France, with the new method of photo-engraving to help them, may be said to have made it the art it now is. You have but to place a drawing of Fortuny's or Menzel's by one of Michael Angelo's or Raphael's to realise how completely modern pen draughtsmen have broken away from the old limitations, and shown that the pen can be used for something more than the mere sketching of projects and intentions. As Mr. Hamerton says, pen drawing is a painter's process, and nearly all these artists were or are great painters as well as great pen draughtsmen.

Fortuny's chief innovation in methods was, as Mr. Hamerton also points out, the use of short broken lines. He adds that Fortuny preferred them probably because he wanted to get variety, and because he saw nothing in nature "that could be fairly interpreted by a long line." But a far more likely reason is that he found with short lines he could model and break up the mechanical look often given by long conventional lines—though all lines are conventional. Fortuny's drawings are full of the most delicate modelling; his figures, instead of being simply and strongly suggested as in the pen sketches of the old masters, are as carefully worked in as if with a brush, and their strength is increased rather than lessened by this care. Mr. Hamerton asserts that the apparently "coarsest pen drawings are usually the work of great artists; the delicate and highly-finished are usually the work of amateurs, or else of workmen who are paid to imitate engravings for the purpose of photographic reproduction." True as this was in a certain sense, it shows that Mr. Hamerton did not foresee the development of photo-engraving, and it is misleading, since nothing could be more delicate and less suggestive of engraving than the drawings of Fortuny. They are moreover full of the most wonderful brilliancy. It was in Africa that his eyes were opened to the strong effects of light and shade under a hot sun, and the desire to reproduce these effects had much to do with his breaking away from academical traditions to originate and develop new methods.

One cannot study too long, too carefully, or too lovingly, the unfortunately few examples of his work which Fortuny has left to us. These are to be found scattered in the illustrated papers of France and Spain, for which he occasionally worked. Poor as were at first many of the reproductions, mostly woodcuts, they stood out from the other work, just as one of his pictures will when by chance it makes its way into an exhibition. His drawings may also be found reproduced in some of the lately published lives of the artist, notably in that by Davillier, his great friend. Here and there in other of Davillier's books are a few of Fortuny's drawings of bronzes and of Spanish and Moorish trappings. The woodcut reproductions, however, are not to be studied, for fine as a few are, notably Leveille's of the portrait of M. D'Epinay in the fashion of Goya's time, the feeling of pen and ink work is in them cut out to a great extent. It is best to see direct reproductions or the photogravures that have been made. It may be asked, How is one to know the difference between woodcuts and process reproductions? This is difficult to explain. In the former there are little dots and engraved lines which can, after some practice, be detected, at times only through the magnifying glass; while the fine grey lines made with a pen are nearly always much harder and broader.[1] Fortuny lived a little too soon for the processes by which his followers have profited. Otherwise there would doubtless have been a still greater number of beautiful pen drawings as well as fine reproductions from them. As it is, many of the process reproductions give his drawings a rough and hard look, which the photogravure reproductions in Davillier's Life prove most conclusively to have been the fault of the undeveloped process.

I have spoken as if Fortuny was the leader of the new movement in Spain. There is very little doubt that he was; but he gave his time almost entirely to painting, and though his few drawings prove him to have been a master, he did not devote himself to the development of pen drawing to the same extent as did some of the other men who worked with and around him. However, Fortuny is known to the whole world as a pen draughtsman, but, owing to the persistent way in which black and white work has been ignored by critics and artistic associations, especially in England and America —notwithstanding the fact that it is the only healthy art developed in the nineteenth century,—the names of the men who have made illustration what it now is, and whose work is studied by intelligent illustrators the world over, are absolutely unknown even to the many who are flooding the world with pen drawings. And yet, men who have studied Rico, Fortuny, and Vierge, are thought to be masters, and their work is praised as being original, when originality is the last merit they would claim for it.

As a landscape pen draughtsman, there is not and has not been

[1] This difference can easily be seen by comparing the drawing by Rossetti, which is a woodcut, with the other heads done by process, given in the explanatory chapter, "Some Comparative Heads: Old and New."

in any country or time a greater man than Martin Rico. Though it may be information to many, Rico, co-worker with Fortuny, is living to-day, still producing those beautiful pen drawings of the canals of Venice and the palaces of Spain which are the admiration of all who know them. He is almost faultless as a draughtsman, and can on white paper with pen and ink catch the sunlight of a Venetian day and the glitter and transparency of a moving, shimmering canal. He understands the true limitations of his art and never goes beyond them ; he knows just where to put a blot of colour and where to leave it out. With his wonderful facility, he can do what seems an impossibility : fill a piece of white paper with modelling, and make a brilliant black with six grey lines. Everything he touches glitters and shines with sunlight, and there is not one superfluous stroke in his drawing ; neither is a necessary line omitted. How true he is only those can realise who have reverently studied him in the countries alone adapted to glowing, glittering, out-of-door pen work—that is in Spain, Italy and Southern France, Africa and the East. Abortive attempts to follow this great master are almost daily made by people ignorant of his work, of the scope of pen drawing, and the reasons for a brilliancy that does not exist north of Southern France and Italy. It is perfectly true that on a summer day some of the little white-washed villages of England and many towns in the United States, especially in the south, are not without the brilliancy best reproduced by the methods of Rico. But how much better it is for the English artist, in a country where these effects are the exception and not the rule, to strike out in a new direction for himself, as has been done, for example, by Alfred Parsons and George Reid, two of the very few British landscape pen draughtsmen of originality. Rico's work is very difficult to find. Many of his original drawings are never reproduced, but are bought up immediately by collectors to be given an honourable place in their galleries. I have seen a number in New York. A few have been reproduced in *L'Art, La Illustracion Española y Americana*, and *La Vie Moderne*.

In fact, the work of these Spaniards must be more difficult to find than I imagined. Although I believe that all real pen draughtsmen know it, an article in *Harper's Magazine*, for March 1888, absolutely failed to mention the work of either Casanova, the best-known Spaniard after Fortuny and Madrazo, or of Vierge, while the writer only refers to some artists who have studied under Rico. This is merely an ordinary example of the utter worthlessness of inartistic art writing.

I think one of the Spaniards who should be ranked with Fortuny and Rico, and indeed above them, as a pen draughtsman and illustrator, is Vierge, a man who has all the draughtsmanship of Fortuny and Menzel, the colour and brilliancy of Rico, the grace and beauty of Abbey, the eccentricity and daring of Blum, Brennan, and Lungren; in a word, a man who, in the few short years of his working life, has proved himself the greatest illustrator who ever lived. I rank Vierge thus above Fortuny and Rico because he has devoted himself more entirely to black and white work.

He flashed out upon the artistic world in a few drawings in *La Vie Moderne*, *Le Monde Illustré*, the Spanish papers, and *The Century* (then *Scribner's Monthly*); in many books, some comparatively commonplace, but one, the most brilliantly illustrated work ever published, which illness, however, prevented him from finishing. Before the illustrations for *Pablo de Ségovie* were all made, his right side and right hand were paralysed, and he lost the power of speech. But when a man is as great as Vierge, his career is only checked, not stopped by a misfortune that would have killed another less strong. A few months after this attack, we find him learning to draw by painting with his left hand—and painting with a cleverness unknown outside of this group of Spaniards. Even the French were so struck with this astonishing marvel, as they called it, that in the papers of that time are to be found drawings of Vierge sitting out of doors, beginning to paint with his left hand. Now he is slowly regaining the use of the right, but still works with the left.

Vierge seems to have learnt everything and to have mastered that cleverness, or the knowledge of how to use one's ability, which is indispensable to good pen drawing, an art only for so-called clever men—men who are interested in their work and who, to attain their ends, are ready, if necessary, to use other than conventional methods, or to get other than commonplace results by ordinary means. If the pen draughtsman who thinks he has discovered some new method looks in that wonderful book, the history of *Pablo de Ségovie*, he finds that Vierge discovered it long before him, and can give him a few new hints into the bargain. You cannot examine the smallest drawing in his masterpiece of illustration without seeing how much study prepared the way for its brilliancy and grace.

Such an influence did this book have upon French pen drawing, that after its publication an entire school of pen draughtsmen following Vierge appeared, and their work was more clever than that of any other draughtsmen, though it did not equal the drawing of their master. Among these men are Ferrand Fau, L. Galice, V. Poirson, and F. Lunel. Their drawings can be seen in the early numbers of *La Vie Moderne*,[1] a complete file of which is to be found in the South Kensington Museum. At the present time, however, this paper is artistically worthless.

Daniel Vierge must not be confounded with his very talented but less brilliant brother, who signed his name S. Urrabieta, while Vierge always omits the Urrabieta and simply signs himself D. Vierge. His brother died recently.

In the Fortuny group, for originality Casanova must be given a very high place—indeed, one almost equal to that of Fortuny himself. I have not seen any large photogravures, or even any very good reproductions of his drawings. They could hardly be engraved on wood, and in the more or less rough and almost cruel reproductions for the *Salon* Catalogue and in French illustrated papers they necessarily lose enormously. The best are in *L'Art*. But even in the poorest reproductions can be seen the exquisite modelling of a monk's head or a woman's hand, the wonderful sparkle of a tiny jewel. His delicate grey lines would be lost in any ordinary attempt at a woodcut.

In the list of the Spanish-Italian school of figure draughtsmen, Madrazo, Fabrès, and a host of others, hold a high rank. But to describe their work in detail would be endless repetition. There is nothing to do but to study it for one's self. To-day the Spanish and Italian illustrated papers are full of the work of imitators of the greater men who revolutionised the whole art of France and Italy—work with which the pages of these papers glitter and sparkle and glow, though it is without the originality of Fortuny, Casanova, and Vierge.

[1] Also see *Les Premières*, the French theatrical journal, *Paris Illustré*, etc.

To speak of an Italian school separately would be impossible, since all alike these children of the sunlight, as they might be called, spend their winters in Paris, Rome, or Madrid, in the life schools or doing nothing, while in summer they find their work out of doors in Spain, Southern France, Italy, or Africa. Senzanni, whose decorative compositions are most charming and graceful, Paolocci, Chessa, Scoppetta, Fabbi, all have a style and character which is well worth study, although it has been founded on that of the great Spaniards. Men like Ximenez, Michetti, Tito, Favretto, Raffaëlli, Gomar, Montalti, whether born in Italy, Spain, or France, as artists can hardly be said to have any nationality. The sun is their god, and Fortuny and Rico are his prophets. Another reason for not speaking separately of Italian pen drawing is, that the greater number of Italian papers and books are so badly printed that the principal pen draughtsmen strive to get their work into French publications, which are not only better made, but appeal to a much larger audience.

The work of the Spanish school may still be a problem to critics who, though they admit its brilliancy, think it all wrong and stupefying because of its contradiction to their preconceived notions of art, it never seeming to occur to them that perhaps their notions, and not the methods criticised, are at fault. But all artists with technical knowledge and broad opinions have recognised new masters in these innovators whose influence has continued steadily to increase.

SPANISH AND ITALIAN WORK

ILLUSTRATIONS

MARIANO FORTUNY

THE full name of Fortuny is José-Maria-Bernardo, but as he dispensed with the greater part of it, we may as well follow his example. He was born in 1838 at Reus, a little town in the province of Tarragona, where he lived until the age of fourteen years, attending the village school. Then his grandfather proposed that they should start out to seek their fortunes, and they footed it to Barcelona. I make these bare statements about Fortuny's early life—statements which are usually the backbone of all art books—simply because I wish to show, first that Fortuny was born years after Menzel, and secondly, that, though this would seem as if from the beginning he had been influenced by Menzel, as were all northern artists, he most probably knew nothing about the great German's work until he went to Rome in 1857.

But there, when studying in the Academy, in the course of the ordinary academical training he most likely, as his biographer Yriarte, who knew him well, says, came under the influence of the followers of Overbeck. I have not the slightest doubt that these Germans possessed examples of Menzel, if indeed at the German embassy or some of the Roman libraries was not to be found a complete set of his already published drawings, which certainly must have been making a profound sensation among the students of that time. Fortuny, not having yet worked out a style of his own, doubtlessly was equally influenced by the drawings of Menzel, the like of which had never been seen before. The chances are, drawings by Fortuny showing this influence might somewhere be found. But just then, war breaking out between Spain and Morocco, Fortuny went off with a Royal Commission to paint on the spot.

It was here in Morocco his eyes were opened to the wonderful effects of light and shade—effects which Menzel had never seen, and had therefore never tried to render. Just as Menzel, influenced by all the old men who, as far back as Bellini, as I have shown, had produced occasional pen drawings which were wonderfully fine, was the first man to take up pen drawing and seriously work at it to express his ideas—why I do not know unless because of an innate love of the medium; so Fortuny, when he got to Africa and back again into Spain, discovered that here was a method by which he could give not only modelling with Menzel, but the brilliancy of sunlight as well. Though, as I have said, he lived too soon for the processes which have enabled his followers to improve on his methods, at the same time we owe all the brilliant work of the modern Spanish school to him.

Fine as is the drawing which I show, I cannot help thinking that the drawings done by Fabrès and Blum, which also are in this book, made years afterwards for process and with a full knowledge of the means to be employed and the results to be obtained, are of more value to the student; because there is in this drawing of Fortuny's the freedom of a master which in the student would merely lead to carelessness, while the background and the floor are worked over so much that, without a vast amount of intelligent hand-work, no process block could reproduce the lines. Knowing some of Fortuny's original work, I fancy that in this block a great many of his delicate greys have been lost. Had he lived later I have no doubt he would have somewhat modified his style, as Vierge has done, to meet the requirements of process. Just as in the Blum plate one can see the texture of the coat with its gold lace and silk lining, the shine of the silken breeches and stockings and the polish of the shoes, so one can study these same indications of texture in the Fortuny block. But when you come to the face you find that it is almost impossible to follow the lines, they having been made probably with grey ink, the back of a quill pen, or anything to be had, without thought of reproduction. The effect is right, but one cannot altogether commend the means by which it has been obtained; in fact the drawing was done for study and not for reproduction. But if this is all we have, we ought to be only too thankful for a drawing which has had so much influence on pen work.

I have explained elsewhere why I have not given a photogravure from Fortuny's work. To me, this block shows it as well as could any other reproduction. There are photogravures in Davillier's *Life*, but they are scarcely important enough to use again. Among the other well-known reproductions are the engraving by Leveille, which does not show the work at all; a very good process block in the *Magazine of Art*, and other blocks in *L'Art* and *La Vie Moderne*, and in Davillier's books. Beyond these I know of very few published examples of Fortuny's work. I have no doubt he made hundreds of drawings, but they would probably be found in the portfolios of his friends.

Finally, what I say is not merely my opinion but that of the men who have devoted their lives to pen drawing. Only the other day I saw in the artistic end of a journal a statement to the effect that the opinions of artists are of no value, and that only the thoughts of the critics are worth preservation. How-

ever, the opinions of Vasari, Sir Joshua Reynolds, and Lalanne, have had some influence on the development of art-work. Just as Sir Joshua Reynolds was opinionated enough to believe that the men of the future would look upon the art of his day as he looked to the art of the Red Indians or the Byzantines, so pen draughtsmen believe that these same men of the future will look to the pen work of Menzel and Fortuny, as we look to the paintings of Giotto and Cimabue.

DANIEL VIERGE

As Menzel is responsible for the development of pen drawing in Germany and England, so is Vierge for the present style and the great advance in technique of draughtsmen in France, Italy, Spain, and America. I know that Vierge falls apparently under Sir Joshua Reynolds' condemnation of superficial cleverness. But when a man draws with Vierge's knowledge and adds to it his skill in handling, his work is something vastly more than clever, although every line might seem to deserve this condemnation. Because Vierge is followed by a number of men in France, Italy, Spain, and America, who, if they lack a certain amount of his inventive cleverness, have added to it much that is original of their own,—although I admit they would never have worked after his manner had he not led the way,—a certain number of critics, and artists too, jump to the conclusion that anybody can do this sort of work. Yet the fact remains that the number of these clever men has not increased, nor have any other draughtsmen been able to supersede them. They in their turn have had their imitators, men without the slightest knowledge of the means used by Vierge to obtain his effects, but no one, even among Vierge's immediate followers, has yet succeeded in surpassing him.

Vierge doubtless owed much to Fortuny. The greater part of his work, and certainly the most characteristic, is done with pen and ink, and, like Fortuny, he uses the pen to fill his drawings with delicate modelling. But however much he learned from his great countryman, he brought to his work a strength, a

delicacy, and a character that were all his own. From the beginning there was no mistaking it for that of any other draughtsman. Not that it is in the least mannered; in looking over the pages of *Pablo de Ségovie* one is struck with the entirely different methods used in the many drawings. With this cleverness of technique one finds the most perfect modelling in the tiniest figures and faces, the most artistic rendering of architecture, the most graceful suggestions of landscape; and the assured touch of the master stamps each and every drawing with individuality.

To get the refinement given in the beautiful little cuts from *Pablo de Ségovie*, it is necessary to make one's drawings very large and yet at the same time to work with the greatest amount of delicacy. For instance, the photogravure is made from a drawing nineteen by twelve inches. The consequence is that in the shadows, which are seemingly put in with such wonderfully delicate lines, though these were delicately drawn, as the drawing was so large the refinement was produced with no special difficulty. There is next to no cross-hatching except in Vierge's later work done since his illness, of which the photogravure is an example, and therefore his drawings can be reduced to almost any extent without the lines filling up. Still, in the volume of *Pablo de Ségovie*, the blocks were almost too small to do full justice to his work, as any one can see by comparing them with the larger reproductions here given and with the plate. Then, again, when he wishes to get a rich colour, he uses a positive black, in the reproduction of which there is apparently no change, although it is a perfectly well-known fact that the whites of any reproduction grow whiter and the blacks blacker as the size decreases. Another quality to be noted in his work is the amount of colour suggested without the use of it. In the plate there is no pure black at all.

There is really very little to be said about Vierge's drawings, except to advise the student to study them in the most thorough manner, and to remind him that their cleverness and apparent freedom is the result of years of the hardest study, and, in each drawing, of days and sometimes weeks of the most careful work. After all I have said, it is almost useless for me to repeat that the effects of light and shade in Vierge's work, being intended for Spanish or southern subjects, are of course utterly out of keeping in drawings made in England. But the cleverness, the skill, is never out of keeping, and the nearer it can be approached, the better for the pen draughtsman and the art of pen drawing.

I know quite well that the most slovenly attempts to imitate Vierge are constantly made and daily applauded; but if you have any real feeling and love for the art, you will, in studying his work, seek, not to make a direct imitation, but to introduce his beauty of drawing and brilliancy of handling into your own, remembering always that such drawings are not knocked off in a morning.

G. FAVRETTO

THIS is only a simple study from one of Favretto's pictures, I think. I use it here to show how much colour can be suggested with very little work. Any one can see that the figures stand in front of a bright, sunlit, glittering wall, and yet there is no work in it at all. The plant, which tells so well against this wall, the bright colours of the flowers, and the still more brilliant tints of the kerchief about the girl's neck, are all rendered charmingly, to any one who can feel them, in this little pen study. To me it is just as much Favretto's work as one of his Venetian paintings. The only thing to be regretted is that we shall never have any more of it. Favretto died but a little more than a year ago.

J. F. RAFFAËLLI

THIS is an excellent example of a simple direct, straightforward drawing of a head. The greater part of it, I should say, was drawn with a quill. The bony formation of the head is remarkably well rendered, and yet, as it should be, in the simplest manner possible. Notice how Raffaëlli has drawn the tassel by a flat mass, and still made it look round, and kept its proper relation and form. Notice too how the stubby beard and the lines of the face are drawn to show the growth of the beard and the direction of this growth, and to express the construction of the face; and only one set of lines is used. Raffaëlli's work is very like Herkomer's. Indeed it is much more like German work than Italian.

A. MONTALTI

THIS is a drawing from *C'era una Volta*, a book of Italian fairy tales published by the Fratelli Treves of Milan in 1885. The whole book is a proof of the possibilities of pen work on grained paper, of which I speak in the Chapter on Materials. There is no possible comparison to be made between Montalti's drawing and the head of De Lesseps by Ringel.[1] That is a pure exercise in the rendering of a low relief; this is an example of artistic decoration applied to book illustration. Not only does it illustrate a passage in the story, but it is given with the greatest amount of decorative feeling, and in a style which goes to prove that there is no reason why we should be dependent on the decorative methods of other times. Conventional forms, of course, are the property of the whole world. It may be argued that there is no meaning in this decoration. Neither to me—and I am sure I speak for all artists who have any honesty in their opinions—is there meaning in nearly all decoration except that of pleasure in the beauty of the design itself. We may be told in Smith's *Classical Dictionary*, or in any of those useful cribs much affected by the intellectual artist, that such and such mysterious swirls and scrawls mean life and immortality, but we are not impressed by this hidden meaning; we only look to see if the line is gracefully drawn.

Montalti's decorations at the side and top of his drawing are graceful. They may have been derived from old iron-work or from his inner consciousness—I do not care from which. The result is pleasing and restful. The white circle behind the girl may be a swirl of life or the bull's eye of a target; but it really is a proof that Montalti is an illustrator who knows the requirements of his art. He has used this white circle for his mass of light which draws attention to the figure of the girl; the figure of the piping shepherd is his great black, and the positive black and white really neutralise each other. It also may be said that the half-decorative, half-realistic daisies at the bottom of the drawing are out of place: nothing is out of place in art if the result is good, and it is nobody's business but the student's how it is obtained. This statement, of course, seems to necessitate the abolition of art critics. But all I can say is that those who criticise art without ever having studied it, have more assurance than it has entered into the brain of any but an art critic to conceive.

The drawing was made on the Fratelli Treves tinted paper, on which I have worked, but at that time it was not so good as the *Papier Gillot*. The original paper can be seen in places where the mechanically-ruled horizontal lines are visible. The positive blacks in the decoration, for example, were probably put in with a pen first, as well as in the figure and the flowers, which

[1] See French Illustrations.

probably were done with both pen and brush. Having gotten in his darks, Montalti scraped with an eraser or pen-knife the light round the shepherd, and thus made a lighter tone by means of cross-hatching, bringing out a perpendicular line in the white. He then obtained his high lights by scraping with

much more force, and removing all the tint from the paper, as in the circle and in the white blots of the decoration. In some places he very probably used Chinese white, because you will often find in working on this paper that after scraping it, if you again attempt pen work, you will be sure to get blots. The drawing cannot be reduced very much in size, while to obtain any but mechanical results is difficult.

ANTONIO FABRES

THIS is not only a masterpiece of feeling for pen work, but a remarkable example of reproduction. Published in *L'Art* a few years ago, and drawn in 1879 in Rome, of course under the influence of Fortuny, this drawing not only surpasses anything Fortuny himself did, but has exerted an enormous influence on pen drawing. I have no hesitation in saying that Fortuny never made a drawing which can approach it for technique, although any one comparing it with the *Man Reading* on another page will see a great similarity. Fortuny has just as carefully studied the man's embroidered coat as Fabrès has the peasant's breeches. But Fabrès' rendering of the texture of the coat, the vest, and the trousers of the peasant, reproduces much more perfectly than Fortuny's work, and this is the point to be noted. Again, Fabrès' head is better than the Fortuny, and he has boldly drawn the hands which Fortuny shirks. To me, at least, his rendering of the whole is more successful than Fortuny's. But Fortuny, being the original man, is responsible for Fabrès, just as Fabrès is for half the French and American illustration of to-day.

How is this drawing done? The greater part of it, including the most delicate modelling of the head and hands and legs—in fact everything, but part of the hat and coat and a little of the hair, is drawn with a pen. The coat and all the hair may have been drawn by a pen by dragging it in various directions, allowing all the ink to run into a blot, and then lifting some of it off with the finger or with blotting paper. The hat most likely was drawn with a brush or with an inked thumb, the background with both, in a manner I have elsewhere described. On these flat tints, the rouletted effect, that is the effect of wash, has been produced by a roulette in the hands of a photo-engraver who is an artist. But this example is the most successful result I know of a very unreliable experiment on the part of the draughtsman. With any but a most skilful artistic workman, the result is certain failure. I am very sorry that the photo-engraver's name is not on the print. I should be glad to give him full credit for his surprising success. The printing of such a drawing is extremely difficult. Do not imagine that the apparently wildly-scrawled background is composed of nothing but wild scrawls. It is indication and suggestion, every bit of which is put down with a purpose. Notice how the background grows out of the deep shadows of the coat, and how the wash and pen work are combined in the shadows between the legs; how the wash work in places is reinforced by pen work, as on the left side near the coat sleeve, and how wonderfully the effect has been reproduced. There are other drawings by Fabrès in *L'Art*,[1] notably a photogravure of a Moor with a gun over his shoulders. But I do not think any of them compare with this.

[1] Also see *Illustrazion Artistica.*

LOUIS GALICE AND FERRAND FAU

THESE charming little drawings give a good idea of the work of two followers of Vierge. The drawing in both is excellent, but it is easy to see that the artists, who would probably be the first to admit it, are inspired by their great master Vierge. The work of men of this school can be seen any week in *Paris Illustré, Les Premières, Le Monde Illustré;* in fact, they are the pen draughtsmen of France to-day. But I have given so much space to the master that it would be only repetition, beautiful as is their work, to dwell upon the followers.

MARTIN RICO

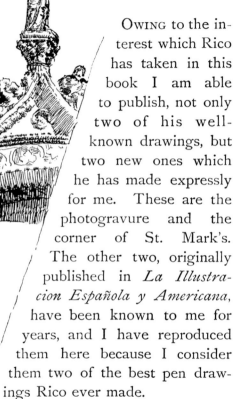

M RICO

OWING to the interest which Rico has taken in this book I am able to publish, not only two of his well-known drawings, but two new ones which he has made expressly for me. These are the photogravure and the corner of St. Mark's. The other two, originally published in *La Illustracion Española y Americana*, have been known to me for years, and I have reproduced them here because I consider them two of the best pen drawings Rico ever made.

The great beauty of Rico's work is the grace of his line, and the brilliancy and strength of light and shade which he obtains with comparatively little work. Not only is there not a superfluous stroke in his drawing, but each line is used, either singly, to express or, together with others, to enforce certain effects he wishes to give. In bright sunlight, the characteristic of Italy and Spain, all his drawings and paintings are made. In the photogravure, the fact of sunshine is not more evident than the actual position

of the sun directly behind the spectator, shown by the direction of every line which goes to make up a shadow. Notice how he has concentrated his only pure black in the two open windows near the centre of the drawing ; and yet, he has relieved this black by bits of pure white, in one window by the flowers trained across it, in the other by the charmingly-placed patches of sunlight just behind the half-closed shutter and on the rich decorations which he has indicated and which we know so well on many Venetian windows. Notice too the light, giving such value to the darks on both sides of it, which shows through the crack between the window-frame and the shutter ; see how the light and shade are managed on the little shrine and on the wall and window under it, and the way in which the light on one wall is carried into the shadow on the other by the arrangement of the foliage. Everything is toned up from these two blacks ; there is not another pure black of importance in any part of the drawing. The effect is thus concentrated and your eye attracted, as he meant it should be, to the very centre of the composition. You should also study the manner in which he works out to the edges of the drawing, leading you into it by the most delicate and graceful lines. His architecture is only hinted and suggested, but so thoroughly does he know his Venice that an architect could work from his suggestions, while for an artist they are simply perfect of their kind ; the capitals, the decorated mouldings running around the buildings, the under side of the cornice, the little shrine, the balcony with its pots and vines and awning, are all well indicated. Bits of these things in nature were of course as dark as his two windows, but he knows, and every one who wishes to make a good drawing should learn, that force must be reserved for one particular point and blacks must not be scattered, if an effective whole is to be produced.

Rico's knowledge of the necessity of concentration is specially notable in the drawing of the Canal with a gondola, in which the inside of the *felze*, or cover of the gondola, is the only pure black ; but it is so skilfully managed with little touches of white, suggestions of the carving, the window on the opposite side and the lamp, that you do not see it is a pure black, for your eye is carried at once to the keynote to the whole picture—the large door which is really not so black as the gondola, but, because there are here no opposing whites, it seems, as Rico intended, much blacker.

In all his drawings Rico invariably breaks his long straight lines, in each, however, in a different manner. The long mouldings in the photogravure are broken by shadows and by foliage ; in the corner of St. Mark's, pigeons not only add grace, but take away from the monotony which would otherwise, unavoidably, be too prominent in this part of the drawing, and even the water-spout helps to serve the same purpose. In the Canal, the gondolas, sandolas, and other boats carry out the straight lines and break them at the same time, while the suggestion of foliage and the balustrade are done as no one ever did them before Rico ; in the Reminiscence of Seville, the carved balcony, beautiful in

itself, would become monotonous were it not relieved by the drapery thrown over it, by the keynote of black supplied in the head of the leaning figure, and by the stone pine farther along. Note how thoroughly the effect of a glittering hot wall is given by the shadow of one drain-pipe, and how rightly the grille with the flower-pots leads into the drawing.

The amount of expression Rico gets in his rendering of reflections in water, always drawn in a very simple manner, is wonderful. There is absolutely no black in them, except where, as in the Canal, I think it is the result of bad reproduction. And yet the suggestion of the effect of a Venetian Canal is right. Here is a point I wish to note : these drawings are not intended to be pictures or records of transient effects ; they are line drawings made in brilliant sunshine. Do not try to imitate them in countries where the effects they give do not exist.

As to the reproduction, in the photogravure it is as good as I can get it and gives an excellent idea of the drawing. There is a certain rottenness about some of the lines which is not in the original, but their relative value is almost right. The lines which appear very fine are really so, and were drawn either with a very fine pen or the back of the pen Rico was using. The drawing is scarcely reduced. It was made in bluish-black ink on white smooth Whatman paper, and, as far as I can see, with very little pencil work, though, as I have already explained, I have seen Rico making very elaborate pencil drawings. He is a master of this sort of work and can do what he wishes ; but for the student it would be very foolish to attempt such a drawing without preliminary pencil work—even with it, he can hardly hope for such results. However, I know of no better models than these four, but it must be remembered that the photogravure is somewhat hard all over and rotten, and that in the process blocks many of the blacks come from the filling up in the printing and the fact that the lines will not stand alone ; a momentary comparison between the blocks and the photogravure will show how much thicker the lines in the former have become in every part.

To realise the great development of pen drawing it is only necessary to place the drawings of Rico by the side of Braun's reproductions of Canaletto's pen work. Rico's are as much in advance of Canaletto's as his were of the drawings of every one of his predecessors. Both artists are true ; but Rico shows how much more we have learned to express by pen drawing.

The drawing of the corner of St. Mark's has been very well reproduced by Waterlow and Sons. It was a difficult piece of work, but they have succeeded in keeping the character of the original.

E. TITO

Tito is one of Rico's cleverest pupils. He has the power of seeing things for himself, and though he works in Venice, where Rico draws and paints, he chooses different subjects, and his figures are drawn much larger and made more important than Rico's. Looking at this drawing, though one sees at once whence its inspiration is derived, it is also evident that, though he works out his drawings in the manner of his master, his subjects are all his own.

A. Casanova
1876

A. CASANOVA Y ESTORACH

CASANOVA is one of those men who seem to be always amusing themselves with their drawings and experimenting, making a dainty suggestion in one place or elaborately working out a figure in another, jotting down notes or trying a pen in the most fascinating manner on the margin of the paper, and always wandering about over the drawing just for pleasure. But if the student should endeavour to imitate this freedom and to wander in this way before he has gone through the necessary training, his results will probably not be so satisfactory to himself or to the public. For Casanova has told me it takes a long time to make a drawing like the plate, and I can well believe it.

This plate is the first large one I have ever seen in which Casanova's work has been worthily rendered. The large process of the monks is from one of his pictures, and the smaller is apparently made for his own enjoyment. One can say really very little about the way such work is done, but I should imagine it was taken up and worked on, a little here and a little there, just when Casanova was in the humour, part of it done with a fine pen, part with a quill, part with his fingers; in fact it is doubtlessly all experimenting, but the experimenting of a man who is almost certain of the results he will obtain.

I do not publish his drawings so much as examples of pen work to be studied, since it would be almost impossible even to copy him, but rather to show the command over the pen of one of the most accomplished of the modern

Antonio Casanova y Estorach Paris 1888

school of Spaniards—men who have something to say and who say it in a fashion of their own.

Casanova is not an illustrator but a painter who cares very little about the

reproduction of his drawings. He knows that no process save photogravure is yet able to render them, for the fineness of his lines and the greyness of his ink make it impossible at the present time to reproduce his work and print it with type. But it is the work of just such experimenters which advances the technique of the art and its reproduction.   Had it not been for Menzel we probably never should have had good fac-simile woodcutting.   Vierge no doubt has done more than any one else to develop process.   Casanova is one after whom woodcutters and process-workers struggle in vain, but this struggle in the end will perfect woodcutting and process, until we have reproductions which will be as good as photogravures and yet may be printed with type.   The art workmen who look ahead are those who are really of service in the world, the workmen, that is, who understand the methods of the past and can make use of their valuable qualities, but who at the same time can look to the future and make improvements.

GERMAN WORK

GERMAN WORK

IN Germany the greatest pen draughtsman is Adolf Menzel, who, in point of age at least, takes precedence of almost all the modern men. Like Fortuny and Rico, he cut himself loose from academical methods and traditions, and like them he had his eyes opened to see in what a valley of dry bones he had been walking by going straight to nature, though, at the same time, he may be said to be a direct descendant of Holbein and Chodowiecki. I do not pretend to know exactly who or what originated the great movement in pen drawing, but there is little doubt that if, just before the introduction of photo-engraving, men in the south of Europe were influenced by Fortuny, artists in the north were by Menzel. Not only German pen draughtsmen, but some of the most brilliant Americans, Englishmen, and Frenchmen owe much to the study of his work.

A very old man—he was born in 1815—Menzel still lives. His most famous illustrations are in the *Life and Works of Frederick the Great, Germania,* and *La Cruche Cassée.* The drawings for the Life, made on the wood, were given to the best Parisian engravers, but Menzel himself was far from being satisfied with the results, for the reason that these engravers reproduced everything in a mannered fashion, giving theirs and not the artist's idea of the original work. This utter subjection of the artist to a mechanical and inartistic engraver is what ruined the work of many clever young Englishmen of a few years ago. The preposterous idea of getting the engraver's and not the artist's lines, although it must have been disheartening to the latter, had at least the good effect of developing wood-cutting, and photographic reproduction, all over the world.

Menzel was so discouraged by the results obtained by the French engravers that the greater number of his drawings were afterwards given to Germans, who were artists enough to know that they were nothing more than machines gifted with human intelligence and artistic sensibility, and that they should devote the whole of their skill, under the artist's direction, to the absolute subjection of themselves, in order that they might perfectly reproduce his work. Even the best results of this perfect subjection, as exemplified in America by men like Cole, Whitney, Collins, Gamm, and Jungling, in fac-simile line-work, do not equal those of a photographic process when assisted by an engraver of less ability, but still a clever man. Moreover the saving of time by these mechanical processes is enormous. Among the engravers who worked for Menzel on the *Life of Frederick the Great* were Bentworth, Unzelmann, and Albert Vogel. Menzel's efforts to have his own work and not the engraver's given, produced not only a resurrection but a revolution in the art of woodcutting in Germany, and this revolution has spread where-ever fac-simile woodcutting is used. However, the use of wood-cutting in this way, though marvellous in the results produced, will soon become a lost art; but, unlike most lost arts, one we can very well dispense with. With the present art of wood-engraving, that is the translation of tone into line as practised by the really great wood-engravers of to-day in Germany, France, and America, I am not concerned. All that I wish to state is, that when we have a process which will give automatically in a few hours exactly the same result the workman obtains after weeks of toilsome and thankless drudgery, there is no reason why we should not use it. I think I am quite right in saying with every artist, excepting probably the reproductive and therefore the more or less mechanical and com-mercial etcher, that I look forward to the days when wood and all other engravings will again hold the place they held in the time of Dürer, and all drawings that are not suited to them will be repro-duced by some mechanical process. Nobody has felt this more than

Menzel, for his first attempt to do without the wood-engraver is shown in his drawing on stone for the lithographer, either to be directly reproduced, or, later, by photo-lithography. Many French critics have said that the German wood-engravers reproduced his work perfectly. But any one who has had drawings reproduced by wood-engraving knows that it is absolutely impossible for the best wood-engraver to preserve all the feeling of the original drawing, while of course the drawing itself is all cut to pieces, if made on the block.

In his *Frederick the Great*, Menzel, as all real artists do in their work, really developed his talent and genius. He began a student, he ended a master. No illustrator ever had a greater opportunity. In the *Works of Frederick the Great* there are over two hundred illustrations by Menzel, engraved by Unzelmann, Hermann Müller, Albert and Otto Vogel, and this work in thirty volumes was published by the Academy of Sciences of Berlin at the command of Frederick William IV. Nearly all the illustrations had to be made of a certain size, rarely more than twelve centimetres, and they were principally head and tail pieces. But into these Menzel has put some of the greatest black and white art of the century. For example, each one of his little portraits, so full of character, is taken from an original picture, or the most authentic source. We hear a great deal about painters going to the Holy Land and the East to get the background for a more or less unimportant picture, and how their paint-boxes and canvases go wrong. But who hears of the hundreds and thousands of studies made for his *Frederick the Great* by Menzel, or for that matter of the thousands of miles travelled, and the difficulties overcome by the artists of the principal illustrated magazines of the day? Their object is the result which they get, and not the belauding of themselves.

Almost every one who has had royalty for a patron has enjoyed great liberality in some ways, but in others has had to endure almost as great disadvantages. For many years Menzel's work was lost in the thirty volumes of the official edition. This work, to which the artist gave six years of his life, and which he filled with his imagination and knowledge, remained almost unknown to the world at large. Fortunately the Museum at Berlin at length issued a special edition of Menzel's drawings. Now his work is almost as well known in France as in Germany, not long ago an exhibition of it having been held in Paris. Master of his art, he recognises the fact that Germany is not the country for brilliancy of effects, and he aims above all at perfection of modelling and the expression of detail.

Dietz, to say nothing of a whole school of followers, is another of the marvellous German draughtsmen. Within the last three or four years, since the introduction of photo-engraving—and here and elsewhere under this term I of course include photo-lithography—and what is known as the Meisenbach process of reproducing wash drawings, an entire change has been effected, notably in the pages of *Fliegende Blätter*, and in the small illustrated books either published in Munich by the proprietors of that journal, or else illustrated by the artists who work for it. These men, some of whom are not Germans, but Austrians and Hungarians, after studying probably in the Munich Academy, started on the lines laid down by Menzel and Dietz, and have already proved the possibilities of pen drawing in rendering the last fashion in gowns, and the pictorial quality that lies hidden in a dress coat and a pair of patent leather pumps. Their work shows the development of a nineteenth century school, whose only point in common with those of other ages is good drawing. There is in it no affectation, or imitation, or endeavours to reproduce bygone methods ; but it is a healthy growth brought about by men who feel and know that the work of to-day can, in its own way, equal that of any other time, and it is their aim to show this in a style of their own. Such books as Hackländer's *Trouville, Ein Erster und ein Letzter Ball, Familien Concert, In der Ardennen, In Damen coupé, Zwischen Zwei Regen*, are, in their turn, like the work of Menzel and Fortuny, influencing the whole world of pen draughtsmen.

I consider the first of these younger men to be H. Schlittgen, an artist whose improvement and march onward is simply marvellous. I have now before me drawings made by him in 1884, 1885, and 1886, and there is no comparison between those of 1886 and those of 1884. Instead of improving backward, like so many illustrators, he is going forward with every book. For the pictorial quality of German life in the nineteenth century, one has only to look for his drawings every week in *Fliegende Blätter*. His work is simple, direct, and right to the point, and everything is drawn with a feeling for its artistic effect. Not a line is wasted. In Hackländer's *Humoristische*, there is on page 5 the study of an advocate, which rivals in simplicity, directness, and expression, anything Randolph Caldecott ever did, and the drawing is infinitely better. The drawing on page 9 of a girl is almost perfection in its rendering in blacks and whites of a modern dress, and no one has ever done anything as full of character as his pompous German officers. For expression and colour, combined with the least amount of work, nothing can be found to surpass the drawing on page 19 of *Trouville* of the interior of a railroad carriage.

H. Albrecht's work is almost as good as that of Schlittgen, but he does not use his blacks and whites with the same strength and vigour. This can also be said of F. Bergen, who, to my mind, puts rather too much work in his drawings. One of the most independent of these Germans, a man who works much more like a Frenchman or an Italian, is Ludwig Marold.

Hermann Lüders and Robert Haug do for the German soldier of to-day that which Menzel did for the soldier of Frederick the Great's time, and they have an advantage which Menzel did not enjoy—direct reproduction. Their work is quite equal to and much more varied than anything of De Neuville's and Detaille's.

Though Germans are traditionally supposed to be somewhat stolid and phlegmatic, there is no doubt that they are the funniest of comic draughtsmen. When the art of a nation is so expressive that one has only to see to understand it, it becomes a universal language. Oberländer's and Busch's drawings at a glance can be understood by the civilised, and, for that matter, probably by the uncivilised world. Like much of Randolph Caldecott's work, there is nothing in Busch's to study for technique. The greater part of it is as slight as the funny and charming sketches Caldecott put in his letters to his friends. Indeed, Busch's work is a perpetual letter to the whole world, which one who runs may read. You cannot look at it without bursting into roars of laughter. The books which appeal to me as much as anything Busch has done, though he has made thousands of drawings, are *Max and Moritz*, in which there is a colour wash over the pen drawing and *Fiffs der Affe*. Oberländer's work, on the contrary, is careful and serious. I only know it in wood blocks, but many of these, like the famous Bad Pen and the Doctor, are equal to Menzel at his best. Oberländer and Busch are only two among a hundred comic draughtsmen. Whoever cares for the work of these artists should study not only

Fliegende Blätter, but their little books which are continually being published.

Englishmen, and especially Americans, congratulate themselves continually on the cleverness of their pen draughtsmen and illustrators. But, as a matter of fact, no cheap book has ever been published in America, or illustrated by English or American artists, that can be compared with the German publications I have just mentioned. The sooner therefore we get to know the work of German pen draughtsmen, carefully studying it and applying it to our own country, or the country where we may happen to be,—though this admission may be very damaging to our own good opinion of our work,—the nearer will our magazines come to being, what we are pleased to think them, the best illustrated publications in the world. It may be interesting to know that some of those wonderfully illustrated books are published and sold for sixpence, while the most expensive cost the enormous sum of a shilling.

Adolph Menzel del: — Octob: 1845. Original in the possession of the Konigliche National-Gallery Berlin.

GERMAN WORK

ILLUSTRATIONS

ADOLF MENZEL

I HAVE made every endeavour to obtain a new drawing from Menzel, but I regret to say my efforts have only resulted in, to me, an interesting correspondence which shows, that in the short working time still remaining to him, he feels that unfinished work already planned must be completed in preference to the undertaking of new schemes. But the Berlin Photographic Company were good enough to obtain permission for me to reproduce by photogravure the drawing of Blücher from the *Germania*, the original of which was not, with so much of Menzel's work, cut to pieces on the block, but is now in the National Gallery at Berlin. It has never been reproduced, so far as I know, except by a woodcut. Fortunately, however, it is a remarkably good example of his style, for even though Menzel did revolutionise illustration and bring again to life fac-simile woodcutting, like all other masters who have devoted themselves to developing any branch of art, he has suffered for those who have followed him in every part of the world. I do not know of but one other photogravure ever made from his pen drawings, and I have seen very few process blocks from them. Charles Keene has shown me two or three lithographs, which he owns and which are apparently *menu* cards and programmes done by Menzel for his friends, and one or two small very clever little drawings, all of which have been reproduced by photo-engraving. I do not know, nor does he, where they were published. An almost parallel case is that of Meissonier, who also devoted many years to illustration, and yet in the numberless books he has illustrated I have only been able to find one photogravure from a pen drawing. But Meissonier has given up illustration, while Menzel has been and always will be primarily an illustrator.

Menzel's pen work began, I believe, with his drawings on stone for the lithographer, and though much of his early work on the stone is absolutely of no value to the student, there is at least one book illustrated with drawings made in this way with a pen and afterwards coloured, I think by hand, which every student should know: this is his *Uniforms of the Army of Frederick the Great*, produced while he was occupied on the *History* and the *Life* and *Works* of Frederick, and *Germania*.   The drawings, three of which I have here given, are simply studies of costume—indeed, one might say, nothing more than fashion plates which show the cut of the clothes of Frederick's army, but such fashion plates as had never before been done in this world.   Instead of the ordinary stupid display of mere costume without the slightest artistic feeling for the subject, every drawing is a portrait of a model, and every one of these models is, not a lay figure to hang clothes on, but a live man. The drawing of the sentinel shows the cut of the front of his coat perfectly, and what more could you want? the make of his gun, the way he carries his accoutrements, and yet, though but a fashion plate, note that he is not stupidly standing just to show his coat, but is plainly a sentinel on duty, yawning with the bored expression a man in his position would probably have.   This or another model can be seen in two or more positions simply to show the back or the side of the same uniform, but always the primary idea is character, expression, action, and not the mere stupid rendering of a coat.   Contrast this bored sentinel with the conceited self-satisfied swaggering drummer who, in the original drawing on the stone, will be found talking to two or three of his companions. I should like to have published a complete plate of these uniforms, but the drawings are so large, each figure nearly as tall as the text of this book, that the whole drawing could not have been put on the page without ruinous reduction.   Technically, I cannot entirely commend either of these drawings, because the very strong and decided blacks which one finds all over them, in the knee of the sentinel, in his coat and his hat, and in the boots of the drummer, were put in to take a colour wash in the book, where they do not tell so strongly as they do here.   But nevertheless, much of Menzel's work does show this impatience with the greying of tones, and a desire to use pure black to get his effect at once and be done with it. This can be seen in the photogravure of Blücher. The head is massive and grand, but the coat is put in carelessly. If I were merely criticising the drawings from the standpoint of the critic I would have no right to object to certain technical details in such master-pieces, since the effect is all right. But this slapdash manner of blotting—not the clever blotting of the Spaniards and Italians —cannot be commended for the student. With him it would only be carelessness; with a master like Menzel, it is an impa-tience with details which he knows he can render if he wants to. For a proof of this, look at the coat of the full-dress uniform of Frederick. The gold lace is worked out as carefully as a mechanical draughtsman would draw the parts of a machine, or a naturalist study the wings of a fly. Note how he has given the set of the coat, the hang of the folds, expressed the colour and sheen of the silk, although the actual colour was put on over it, and do not attempt to say he could not draw detail when he wanted. Why, everything is even mea-sured, and this is only a bit of one of the enormous pages; on the same page there are details of hats and swords and of canes, even down to a measured drawing of the weaving of a sash. But if Menzel were doing these things to-day, I cannot help thinking he would get a better result, for two reasons: these were drawn on the stone with lithographic ink which is, first, a tedious and slow process, and secondly, it is almost impossible to print lines as finely as they were drawn, because, as any one who has tried it knows, lithographic

ink blots easily, or if it does not blot, the result is much thicker and harder and blacker on white paper than the original drawing on the beautifully-toned stone. I really wish to show them as models of expression and good drawing rather than of technique. Personally, I prefer the delicate refinement of Abbey

in this sort of work to the brute strength of Menzel.   Both men can draw
details ; but Abbey seems to love them ; Menzel, though he never slights or
draws them badly, apparently hates to be obliged to do them.   But it must
be remembered that when these drawings were made, Menzel stood absolutely
alone in the world as an illustrator.   I am sure, however, that future generations
will look back to him as the Michael Angelo of illustration.   It is all very well
to say he was influenced by Chodowiecki, whom I believe he acknowledges to
be his master, but Menzel is as much greater than Chodowiecki as Reynolds
was greater than Hudson.   And as I have said in the Chapter on Fortuny, the
sensation his drawings made when they first appeared was so great, I believe
they were what sent Fortuny straight, not to copying them as a weaker man
would have done, but to nature.

In conclusion, I do not want it to be thought that Menzel did not as a rule
draw details.   When working for the woodcutter he used the most marvellous
refinement of detail ; when working for himself, as the illustrator of to-day
works, he was bold and free as these drawings show.   No one has ever
approached the exquisite delicacy of the little head and tail-pieces in the *Works*
of Frederick.   I have not used them because they are all woodcuts.

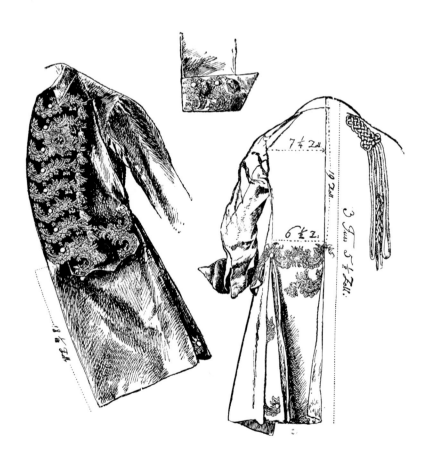

W. DIETZ

I suppose this is by the well-known Dietz of Munich. In the title of the drawing given in *Kunst für Alle*, where it was published, the name was printed Diez. In English publications it is usually spelt with a T. It is scarcely probable there could have been two men of the same name, both working at the same time, and in the same place. The late Munich professor, I know, made any number of illustrations for *Fliegende Blätter*, and I believe this to be one of his drawings. But the design is of great value, and this is really the important point. It shows how well he was able to carry out the feeling of the old Dutchmen with a handling all his own, though it suggests both Menzel and Vierge. Still I cannot help saying that the barrels in the foreground, the drawing of the grass, and the toned side of the house, might have been much better rendered with no greater work. But the group of little figures is, I find, in power and completeness of expression equal to anything in the book. And it is this power of expression, combined with care in the selection of each line, which marks the modern German style of drawing, several excellent examples of which I have been fortunate enough to secure. This thought for line, which interests and fascinates all artists, distinguishes the work of these Germans from the equally simple but utterly careless and thoughtless engraved line of men like Leech and his English followers.

H. SCHLITTGEN

SCHLITTGEN is the best known of all the German draughtsmen, and these two drawings are fair examples of his style. To the simplicity of character sketching of Haug and Lüders is added the use of pure strong colour, as in the dress of the girl in the foreground of the large drawing. There is very little to say, except that his work is very clever and has influenced the pen draughtsmen of the world. The most superficial glance at it will show where many illustrators of to-day have got their style. Notice the charming grouping of the figures, and the action and movement which pervades the whole drawing and which is given in very few lines. Notice, too, the thoughtful placing of the little blacks and whites, their arrangement against each other so as to tell with the utmost effect. Everything in Schlittgen is studied and thought out in the most careful manner.

The large drawing is from *Trouville;* the smaller one, which shows most perfectly what might be called his serious caricature, is from *Ein Erster und ein Letzter Ball,* and is a wonderful rendering of that wonderful creation, the German officer.

All the Hackländer books, from which these are taken, should be seen and studied; the price of each is a shilling, and they can be obtained at Trübner's in London.

ROBERT HAUG AND HERMANN LÜDERS

NONE of the German publications and books, with the exception of *Fliegende Blätter* and the little volumes, I have mentioned, illustrated by the artists of that paper, have a very wide circulation among English-speaking people.

While nearly every German city of any importance possesses an art academy, one at least having a world-wide reputation, it is rather strange that a greater number of really good pen drawings are not seen. Though probably there are innumerable Germans who do very good work with a pen, the fact remains that but very few seem to care to, or do, get their work published. I do not know if in Germany there exists a prejudice against the employment of a new man, as I regret to say there does in certain quarters in England. However that may be, only the work of the men here represented is seen to any great extent, and, interesting as it would be to discover work done by the artist for study or practice, it is the object of this book to show the work of men well known as illustrators.

As I have said, Hermann Lüders and Robert Haug are two most notable followers of Menzel, and in the two small drawings here given—all their drawings I know are small—can be seen most clearly their style of work, which is very similar, and which consists of the greatest expression of character given in

the fewest possible lines.   Contrast the light dapper officer in Lüders's drawing
of a review, in *Ein Soldatenleben*, with the heavy files which are passing.
Although the drawing is almost in outline, you can see the different quality of
the cloth in the officer's and in the privates' uniforms, and every soldier's face
has a character of its own, although it may be given in only two lines.   Notice
the curve shown in the feet of the advancing file—the curve which is always
seen in any column of marching men.   To me, at least, the portraits of the
Emperor, the Crown Prince, and Von Moltke, are quite as complete and
satisfactory as any elaborate work in oil, and this small drawing contains as
much character and as much feeling for the artistic quality of line as any etching
that was ever produced.   I know, of course, there would be more refinement in
the etched line, but these two drawings in their way are perfect.

The drawing by Haug of the cavalry passing is from *Ein Schloss in den
Ardennen*, and of it, especially of his drawing of horses, exactly the same things
may be said as of Lüders's work.   Both of these books—and it may here be
noted that *Ein Soldatenleben* is written as well as illustrated by Hermann
Lüders—should be known and studied, as well as Vierge's *Pablo de Ségovie* and
Abbey's and Parsons's *Old Songs*, by all who wish for style and care for the best
results in pen drawing.   These drawings were reproduced in Vienna.

LUDWIG MAROLD

MAROLD'S work possesses more of the cleverness of half a dozen Italians, though it is not an imitation of any one of them, than that of any other German I know. The drawing in the hands of the three girls is very careless; but the simplicity of the work combined with the strong bits of colour and the character in the faces makes a whole which is very pleasing and interesting, and which certainly has a style of its own.

A. OBERLÄNDER

OBERLÄNDER is always called a caricaturist, and he is a caricaturist in the true sense of the word, for he shows in his drawings the humorous side of his subject without aggressive exaggeration, and in a manner which interests artists as well as people who have no knowledge of art. The caricaturist who merely puts a little head, a big nose, or long legs to a figure, without drawing it in a good technical style, and expects people to laugh at it, although he may appeal to a vast inartistic public for a moment, because this abomination somewhat suggests a notoriety or celebrity, cannot permanently attract those who really care for art work. Can anything be more wearisome than to go through either one of the histories of caricature or a file of the political comic papers? You turn over page after page only to find the stupid portrayal of forgotten men and unremembered and trivial events. Without the legend accompanying them they are unintelligible, and nearly always the events which led to the publication of the picture are forgotten and all interest in the subject has ceased. The man who puts down such trivialities and the public who appreciate them are not much above the schoolboy who scrawls the effigy of his schoolmaster on a back fence. I do not mean to say for a moment that all caricatures should be as elaborate as this example of Oberländer's work. He and many another man can tell a story in half a dozen artistically disposed lines. But a caricaturist who can work out a drawing, and yet keep in it the comic and amusing element, possesses a power given to few.

I care not for a minute if this is a portrait of a doctor in Berlin or Munich, or only of a model. The subject is of absolutely no importance, but the way in which it is worked out is of the greatest value to artists. I am very sorry that the drawing has been engraved on wood; though it has been very well cut by Roth, in all of the darker parts the pen drawing quality is lost in the woodcut line. But as the drawing was most likely made on the block—at least I have never been able to find out anything about the original—this was all I could give. However, what remains of it, to my mind, reaches the high-water mark of caricature.

Any number of Oberländer's drawings can be found in the German papers, from which they are often taken by the periodicals of the whole world, as they can be understood by every one without a story to explain them.

ALBERT RICHTER

AND

OTHER ARTISTS IN "UNIVERSUM"

WHILE *Fliegende Blätter* and its artists—among whom I probably ought to have mentioned Hengel, who tells his stories all over the page, and Stübbe—are known everywhere, magazines like *Universum, Kunst für Alle, Felz zum Meer, Daheim*, have little, if any, circulation in English-speaking countries. And moreover, it is only occasionally, for a year or six months at a time, that these magazines rise to the level of originality. It has been less a surprise to find my own work in some of them than to discover good original drawings. For though they borrow from all sources, they rarely keep up a high standard in work done specially for them. I have already referred to the series of reproductions by Angerer and Göschl after Rembrandt in *Daheim*, where they made an oasis in a desert of commonplaceness ; in half a ton of *Felz zum Meer*, there is hardly a notable drawing done by a German in pen and ink ; but in *Universum*, at times straight away for a year, one will find a number of good drawings, and then the magazine will degenerate, only to be revived again. All through it, however, there is good decorative work by E. Unger, two of whose very characteristic designs I have included in the Chapter on Decoration. There is Scheyner who draws like Haug, and Mandlick who works like Schlittgen.

But I think the most original of all the men who have illustrated this magazine is Albert Richter, who draws landscape and interiors, and three of whose drawings are given. The expression of detail in the carving over the open doorway and in the corner of the room is very well rendered, while the bit of a German town is extremely characteristic, the German feeling being well kept. The drawings are very slight, but despite this slightness there is evident a great desire to show with the simplest means the most picturesque aspects of very commonplace subjects. In fact they possess the true illustrative quality.

The only other drawings worth notice, except the single Vierge-like drawing by Dietz, the heliotype by Waldemar Frederick, and those of the other men I mention when describing it on another page, are by the military painter Lang in *Kunst für Alle*, from whom very likely Haug, Lüders, and Scheyner got their ideas, but he is not an illustrator and they are.

A. STUCKI

THERE is nothing more difficult to draw with a pen than low relief or decoration, and while Jacquemart, with his books made rare by limited editions, illustrated with etchings and therefore only for collectors and amateurs, gained a great reputation for himself, this man who can draw just as well and with as much feeling for light and shade and colour and the play of reflections on polished surfaces, in which lay Jacquemart's great strength, is unknown because, though he treats the same objects in the same manner, he draws them with a pen. The sole difference is that he works for the people, and Jacquemart, though himself an artistic man, catered to the collector who is usually unable to appreciate his work technically. The chasing and the roundness and the metallic feeling of this cup or chalice could not be better rendered by any other medium. Lately, notably in the *Century* and *Harper's*, there have been published drawings by Will H. Drake which approach, but I do not think equal, this. Drake's work is more artistically put together; his backgrounds have some relation to the objects drawn, this is meaningless. But I do not find that the subjects themselves are as well treated by Drake and the other Americans, that is in feeling for surface and material.

WALDEMAR FREDERICK

UNIVERSUM contains one sort of work which has not been used to very great extent by any other popular magazine. For a year or two it gave a heliotype or photo-print as a frontispiece to each number. The architectural papers have almost always employed some form of this method of reproduction, and it can also be seen in the *Universal Review*. It is very cheap but exceedingly effective, and there is no reason why it should not be more extensively adopted. Among the men whose drawings have been published in this way are Waldemar Frederick, K. Richfelt, and Hugo Kaufman. The pen drawings in which there is a wash come very well by this process, though they cannot be printed with the text. This, of course, is the objection to it. It gives the character of the artist's work comparatively perfectly and is usually printed in two or more colours. The results are not as accurate as those obtained by photogravure, but for the reproduction of wash it is superior to a relief block. The drawings are merely photographed on to a lithographic stone or gelatine film, and printed in a lithographic press. The process is well enough known all over the world with more variety in name than in method. For it is indifferently called heliogravure, heliotype, photo-tint, ink photo, and it is not infrequently palmed off as photogravure. The process is altogether different, a photogravure, as the name implies, being printed from an engraved plate, the heliotype from the surface, as a lithograph.

Waldemar Frederick's drawing of the figure is excellent, and thoroughly German in character, and the reproduction is good, though it seems to me that much must have been lost in the shadows. Of this I cannot be sure, as I have not seen the original drawing. But the prints themselves even in an edition as small as this vary very much, and the want of accuracy in printing is enough to prevent the success of any process as a method for popular illustration.

PEN DRAWING IN FRANCE

PEN DRAWING IN FRANCE

CRITICS have spoken of French drawings as tricky. I am not quite sure what this may mean, but I am certain that in French, as in Spanish drawing, dull mechanical work was done away with, and clever handling took its place. At the same time that the great Spaniards were beginning to be famous, Detaille and De Neuville appeared in France. They studied under Meissonier. A reference to this artist's pen drawings, even though they are engraved on wood, will show that his method of working with a pen was careful, reverent, and accurate. But as he does not illustrate any more, and as I have never seen but one of his drawings reproduced by photo-engraving, there is no more reason why I should speak of him than that I should go back to Vernet, and then to Claude and Nicholas Poussin—in fact to the beginning of French art. As I have said, it is with the pen drawing of to-day, and of no other time, that I am here concerned.

Even before De Neuville and Detaille and Meissonier, Paul Huet had already given signs of the coming change. But his drawings were not known until after his death, when they were looked upon as revelations. Rousseau, when he took a pen, was too careless, or I suppose some would say too old-masterish, to care about line, but he managed his blacks effectively in his wood interiors. Millet, too, worked with a pen, especially a quill, not exactly as the old men did, but still with simplicity, making a few lines tell a whole story. Doré, of course, produced hundreds and probably thousands of pen drawings; but I suppose it is now almost universally admitted that his facility killed his art, as it eventually killed himself. Not only this, but the greater part of his work, was done for the engraver.

Looking at great men like Menzel and Vierge, one is struck by the fact that their original work is expressed by pen drawing. With the majority of Frenchmen, pen drawing has been the means of giving the public an artistic rendering of their pictures in black and white. It has also been used in this way in England, but, as a rule, in anything but an artistic manner. De Neuville and Detaille and hundreds of others drew in pen and ink with the adjunct of wash, not that the pen was to them of any special importance; it simply happened to be the medium that was the fashion. Their sketches were really a working-out of the old projects' and intentions' scheme. With the introduction of photo-engraving, the publication of *L'Art* and the *Salon* Catalogues, and the coming of the Spaniards of whom I have spoken, the revolution began in France. Of course the Frenchmen were ready for this artistic change in their work, and only adapted their style to the new requirements.

In De Neuville's well-known drawings of war subjects, as in Menzel's work, there is the most careful modelling, obtained by simple and direct means, and the utmost refinement. Mr. Hamerton devotes much space to justly praising his *Coups de Fusil*, published by Charpentier, but to praise De Neuville and to omit Detaille is to slight an artist who is no less brilliant as a pen draughtsman. To write of these two men and to omit Jeanniot would be an inexcusable oversight.

In my estimation Jeanniot is the leading French pen draughts-man. He has of course painted, but he is more of a pen draughts-man than a painter, and therefore should be here ranked above these two better-known men who, owing to the magnificent series of photogravure reproductions of their paintings published by Goupil, have acquired a wide-spread popularity. Jeanniot has devoted himself almost exclusively to illustrating the magazines, and showing the French life of to-day. I hardly know where or when he began to draw, but the first numbers of *La Vie Moderne* are filled with examples of his work. Exactly the same can be said of Adrien Marie and Renouard, who are known in England through the *Graphic*. Indeed, the *Graphic*, as it admits, is at the present moment very much dependent on the drawings of these men. Of late most of the work of Renouard, however, is in chalk. Mars also has done much for English papers, with his rendering of life on the sea-shore, and his charming children.

At one time, in almost every number of *La Vie Moderne*, was to be seen work which, though the artists' names might be unknown to us outside of France, was clever and marked with originality. The same can be said of an innumerable host in *Paris Illustré, Le Petit Journal pour Rire, La Vie Parisienne, L'Illustration, Le Monde Illustré, Revue Illustrée, Le Courrier Français;* or if you look any week in books which bear the little card *Vient de Paraître*, you will probably find in their pages some exquisite little gem by a man you never heard of before. Almost every French pen draughtsman has made the books and papers of the day—whether big or little, comic or serious, important or frivolous—beautiful and worthy of study. The early volumes of *La Vie Moderne* and *L'Art* are the best masters that any pen draughtsman could have.

It would really be much easier to name the French artists who cannot draw with a pen than those who can. However, among the better known draughtsmen I might mention Duez, whose brilliant sketches transfer scenes from the theatre to the pages of the theatrical papers; Jean Béraud, who makes wonderful interiors with effects of light and shade; Maurice Leloir, who has given us a new Sterne; Auguste Lançon, whose drawings of animals have an enormous amount of strength and vigour, and who, I believe, has been called the "Cat Raphael"; Lucien Gautier, who can make a bronze statuette or a marble group with the sunlight glowing on it and its soft reflected shadows, real for us in *L'Art;* Bracquemond, the etcher, whose head and tail-pieces are charming, while his little sketches are as wonderful as Japanese work; Ringel, the modeller, who seems able to do anything, and whose drawings after his own placques are the most clever that have ever been made; H. Scott, who is a delightful architectural draughtsman; E. Adan, who renders his own pictures charmingly; Rochegrosse; Mme. Lemaire; Edmond Yon; Robida, who is very popular both as a caricaturist and an artistic traveller; Brunet-Debaines, who was one of the first to show Englishmen what pen drawing for process-reproduction should be; Habert-Dys, who draws an initial or the border of a page with most effective brilliancy by means of almost pure blacks and whites; graceful swallows flit about chimney-pot initials, Japanese dolls tumble all around the text, perfect oriental feeling pervades his head and tail pieces, and all his work is suffused with his own personality.

There is one Frenchman who stands apart from all these men, and who is the landscape pen draughtsman of France. This is Maxime Lalanne, who has recently died full of honours, if not of years. Without his beautiful drawings Havard's *Hollande* would be veritably dead as the cities of the Zuyder Zee. His bird's-eye views have made them live again. For quick, bright, strong, incisive work, for getting at the essence of a thing with sharp, short, brilliant strokes, perhaps no one can equal him. The only possible drawback to his work is that there is too much Lalanne in it. He knew, if anything, too well what he was going to do. He can hardly be called mannered, because a mannered man usually cares nothing for nature with its variety and subtlety, while Lalanne really did care and makes you feel that he cared. I may perhaps best explain what I mean by saying that Rico in his work seems to ask, " Is this the way a tree or a bit of water ought to look? I think it is;" while Lalanne in his is more positive: " This is the way the tree or bit of water looks; I know it," he seems to say. He is almost too sure of himself.

In speaking of French pen drawing one cannot help noticing that a few years ago it was the fashion in Paris to draw with the pen—a fashion, as I have said, started by the Spaniards, then living there. The work of the French artists, although not so clever as that of the Spaniards, was almost all good, simple, and careful. But at the same time the leading attraction of the French magazines and journals was the fact that week after week Vierge, his brother or his followers, or other Spaniards, contributed, as they still continue to do, the most striking drawings. But since the introduction of the Guillaume and Meisenbach processes much of this work has been given up, and only those artists who care for line and the quality to be gotten with a pen still produce pen drawings. What has given that which is known as French art its reputation with art students and art lovers, is the fact that it is not French art at all, but the art of the whole world; for there is not the slightest doubt that the work of the greatest artists of the day is to be seen at one time or another in Paris, which has therefore become the art metropolis. The *Salon* is really the broadest and most varied exhibition in the world, and far less French than the Royal Academy is English.

Almost every French pen draughtsman to whom I have referred is a well-known painter. If you take up to-day a *Salon* Catalogue,[1] you find it full of charming pen drawing reproductions, pictures in themselves. Of these I have given several as examples. Indeed, the list of the greatest pen draughtsmen is, as I said of the Spaniards, the list of the great painters. The fashion of illustrating catalogues commenced, I believe, in France, and grew and developed there under the care of *L'Art* and the publishers of the *Salon* Catalogue until its influence has made itself felt, even in England, though here very little of the French feeling has been retained. The French work is done for the sake of the drawing; the English catalogue is but an inartistic reading book for the artless. There have been some exceptions. Some good drawings have been made for English catalogues, just as of late years the *Salon* Catalogues have been given over to less able draughtsmen, for this reason : at the present moment many of the best known artists are having their paintings reproduced by a mechanical tone process. In some ways this is unfortunate for pen drawing; in others it is fortunate, since it helps to confine pen drawing to its proper sphere, which is not the reproduction of tone, but of line only. The publication of *L'Art* and these catalogues not only created a school of French pen draughtsmen, whose sole work it was to reproduce other men's art, but, so powerful was its influence, that it produced a few English artists, who for a time did very fine work of the same kind, but of them

---

[1] I want to make an exception of the Catalogue for 1887, which is very bad. Some of the drawings may have been good, but over them has been put a grey tone which gives them a uniform cheap look, and, in nearly every case, ruins them. The Catalogue for 1888 is not very much better. The most artistic cheap French Catalogue published, as far as I know, is that of the *Société d'Aquarellistes*.

I shall speak in the English Chapter. It is owing to the same influence that the finest catalogues ever issued have been published in America, and that in that country catalogue-making and advertising have become a fine art.

If the healthy black and white art, which is the art of the nineteenth century, is put into advertisements, catalogues, the daily and weekly papers, journals and magazines, and the people really appreciate, understand, and care for it, as they do in France, Germany, and America, I believe it is doing just as much good as pictures buried away in churches, which they look and wonder at through the eyes of a guide-book or of a religious art teacher, and the beauties of which seeing, they do not perceive, and the meaning of which hearing, they do not understand.

PEN DRAWING IN FRANCE

ILLUSTRATIONS

LÉON LHERMITTE

IN every branch of art work at which I have ever known him to try his hand, Lhermitte seems equally at home. His pictures are always among the most distinguished in the *Salon;* his water-colours are always to be included with the successes at the exhibitions of the *Société des Aquarellistes Français;* his pastels surprise every one who sees them; his charcoal drawings are worked out with a massive and big completeness which proves that this medium can be used for something more than the pretty finicky work to which it is devoted on the one hand, or to the making of slight studies or rapid sketches for which it is so often employed on the other; his etchings of interiors of churches and his west front of the Cathedral of Rouen are known all over the world; and I have now, through the kindness of Messrs. Seeley, the opportunity of properly showing one of his pen drawings.

Although not almost exclusively, like Abbey, an illustrator, or unable, like Menzel, to express himself equally well in colour, he is quite as much at home in the many books and papers he has decorated as they are. There is an entire absence of all cleverness in his work—I mean in the sense in which that of the Spaniards is clever—yet a straightforward way of rendering every subject he attempts makes his drawings most interesting, and he certainly possesses a very strong and marked individuality. Although he does not confine himself by any means to the life of the peasant, as Millet did, all his work which I have seen treats some one or other phase of French life, and is done with the greatest possible endeavour to show the truth about his subject without affectation or exaggeration. The drawing I have reproduced gives one of the old streets in Paris. It is made with blue ink, evidently with an ordinary pen on a piece of very poor white drawing paper, and is handled in exactly the same way as are his etchings. He has endeavoured to show the mass of objects, which fill one of these old rag-pickers' streets in the heart of Paris, without giving undue prominence to any one part, or without any apparent brilliancy of execution. But if the drawing is looked into, it will be realised that every object in it keeps its proper place, while he has suggested not only light and shade by very simple means, but colour as well. He works in his important figures in the foreground, or the objects he wishes to emphasise, by using a broader pen or by greater pressure just as an etcher would ; and at the same time he allows portions of them to sink into other parts of the drawing just as they do in nature. I do not want any one to think I publish it altogether as an example of style, because many of the lines are put in with an effect of carelessness, and it is only when one examines them carefully that one sees they are right. The modelling, which at first is almost hidden, will also be found. But I cannot help pointing out that a drawing, like Abbey's, in which every line is carefully thought about is far better for study. If the student fears that he is becoming too careful with each line—which is really an impossibility—he can easily allow himself greater freedom. But apparently this drawing of Lhermitte's could not be done much more freely. And yet, on looking into it closely, it can be seen that a pencil drawing was originally made under the freest part of the ink work ; it is really only by having a solid groundwork that one can indicate and express the various parts which go to make up a whole as interesting as this. Then of course there is another reason for not working so freely as Lhermitte does here : no process but photogravure would reproduce this work accurately. The original reproduction in Mr. Hamerton's *Paris* gave no idea whatever of the drawing.

There is one quality to be noted, however, in such work. It is unmistakably done out of doors and from nature, with probably little thought about line, and therefore has none of the cut and dried sort of freedom that can easily be distinguished from the genuine thing. Notice how all the forms of the stones and the stains on the wall are given on the left-hand side, and so freely, and yet so carefully, you know they must be facts recorded from nature. Notice how the whites in the men's shirts and baskets tell, not too strongly but just right, and how Lhermitte has indicated the grey misty distance in the old high narrow street. Of course the windows and the doors on the right might have been drawn much more carefully, and the lamp-post which sticks out at the side is very bad. But throughout the whole drawing there is a good honest endeavour to represent a street he has seen, though the way in which this was to be done was of minor importance. With Parsons or with Blum or with Rico, the handling is of no less importance than the subject. These men give as much thought to the reproduction as to any special quality in the drawing. A man like Lhermitte evidently does not, but he knows what he wants to express, and, as I have said in several other places, it is only by working after drawings like his that photo-engraving advances at all.

EDOUARD DETAILLE

NOTHING has been more of a surprise to me in preparing this book than to find how comparatively few pure pen drawings have been made by two men so well known for black and white work as De Neuville and Detaille. I have not forgotten that I have said in another place I myself care little whether a drawing is pure pen work or not, and I have shown other drawings where wash is used with the pen work. But, as I have also said, nothing but a pure pen drawing can be reproduced with so little labour and without hand work. These two men studied under Meissonier before the coming of process, and they drew on the wood; therefore, though their work was well reproduced, it made very little difference whether there was a wash in it or not. During the last decade, in which their reputation has been made, and De Neuville unfortunately has died, though they have done a vast amount of work for reproduction—in fact, almost all their work was intended for this purpose,—it has been for reproduction by photogravure, either in colour or in black and white, from their paintings and not from their line drawings.

There are, of course, a great number of sketches in pen and ink, more or less slight and always interesting, to be had from them like this sketch and the series for the *Coups de Fusil*, which have a great deal of wash in them, and which I do not think were a great success, or else I should have shown one or two here. The accompanying drawing by Detaille is a sketch of the principal figure in the picture called *L'Alerte*, and though it was exhibited, as are hundreds of his and De Neuville's drawings, it is nothing more than a sketch of projects and intentions, but far better than any old man could have done it. The drawing itself is good, and the action and movement of the man and horse are very well expressed. But it is filled with careless blots and smudges. It is the sketch of a master, primarily done for his own use, though he is willing to show it. A glance at the work of Jeanniot or Haug and Lüders will show that Detaille's drawing is a work for study, theirs are works for exhibition. Having studied the methods of fifteen or twenty years ago, and having met with success in other ways, he has never paid the necessary attention to the essentially modern illustrative methods. From his standpoint there is no reason why he should. He paints for reproduction, and in the reproductions published by Goupil, from the cheapest to the most expensive, he does appeal to the people. No one to-day knows more about painting for reproduction than Detaille. He is one of the men who have given up pen drawing because their wash drawings can be reproduced equally well. In his great work, *L'Armée Française*, there are scarcely any pen drawings at all.

MADELEINE LEMAIRE

I AM not yet sure whether I should have selected this charming figure of a flower-girl, or one of Madame Lemaire's studies of flowers, which she renders with more colour and less work than even Alfred Parsons, though I cannot think she gives as much attention to the delicacy of each individual form and the expression of its growth. But there is no doubt whatever to her right to a place as a figure draughts-woman. There is no one living who can approach her for refinement of drawing and rendering of colour in a simple un-affected manner. Louis Leloir was cer-tainly her equal, but I know of no one else. I think she is even superior to Abbey in the suggestion of colour in a single figure. But then Abbey can carry out a drawing more completely, making a picture - illustration, while Madame Lemaire's designs are only notes of her pictures, but notes of a most artistic sort. The principal quali-ties to be studied in her work are the simplicity of line and the grace of handling.

E. DANTAN

THIS drawing shows a consummate mastery of technique in a man who has given the world very little pen drawing—at least very little that I have been able to find. Of course in the original picture the greatest cleverness was manifested in the scheme of light, the posing of the figures, and the arrangement of the different parts. But to suggest this cleverness in pen and ink without over elaboration is quite as wonderful. The reserving of blacks here, as in all other good drawings, will be noted. But the great feature is the rendering of the greys, and especially the flesh tints of the model in the foreground. You feel instinctively the difference between the relief on which the sculptor is working, the little coloured figure, the model herself, and the cloth which carries the light from the relief down her arms on to the box where she is sitting. All of this is produced by the most simple means, and yet the different surfaces are perfectly suggested. It cannot be said there is any great cleverness in the handling; the drawing itself in places might be much better. The model's hands and one of the sculptor's are probably not up to those in the picture. But this drawing should be studied mainly for its suggestion of colour, and for the very careful and, at the same time, very artistic manner in which Yves and Barret have engraved it. The skilful use of cross-hatching has contributed in many places to the successful rendering of the character of the different surfaces. And yet in some of the most difficult passages, notably in the model herself, there is none of this hand work; the whole effect is entirely due to the artist. But right alongside the model, look at the delicate way in which Dantan's name is engraved. It might be remarked that this is too trivial to notice; but it is such apparent trivialities that make the difference between good and bad work.

The outlines of the figure on the relief are somewhat rough and hard. I think they should have been cut down and thus softened. The hardness is probably due to a defect in the block. As it is, the outlines catch one's eye unpleasantly. As to the rendering of the canvasses in high light above the relief, the placques and reliefs on the wall which runs at right angles to it, at the left hand of the drawing, I think the surfaces and the colour and texture suggested are worked out, though unobtrusively, as well as the principal motive in the picture. But every part of this drawing is worthy of the most careful and thorough study.

Dantan assures me that the drawing is his own work, and, as I have said, it is simply wonderful that a man who has shown so little pen work should get such perfect results. I have no doubt that he is responsible in a great measure for the careful engraving, and therefore it is almost presumptuous of me to offer any criticism upon it. This drawing is but another proof of what I have asserted: if an artist can reproduce his own picture in pen and ink artistically, he produces not only a valuable record but a new work of art. It is to this drawing, as much as to the picture itself, that Dantan owes his fame.[1]

[1] For work of this class Emile Adan's *Ferryman's Daughter* and *Autumn* should be seen.

Σ·DANTAN · 1880 ~

PHO. YVES & BARRET.

P. G. JEANNIOT

THE reason I have not given a photogravure to Jeanniot, whom I have called the leading French pen draughtsman, is because his work comes perfectly well by process. He has a style and character of his own, and by the simplest means he obtains the most artistic results. Take this little drawing of the boulevards at night with a *kiosque;* the effect of the light which comes from it, the light of the shop windows, and their reflections on the wet asphalt, are given as well as if the drawing was made in wash. There is no over elaboration and unnecessary work. The tones are suggested in a remarkable manner. Of course they are all wrong, but they give the right effect. In fact, the little drawing which heads this page should be carefully studied.

Then take the drawing of the soldiers drilling. Randolph Caldecott never did a better dog than the one standing in the foreground looking at the officer, and the recruit close by is simply the thing itself. Look at the character in the awkward squad, in all the spectators, in the officers. The houses in the background, however, are careless. They might have been suggested much more artistically with very little more work. But the figures are altogether delightful in their suggestion of character, and every line shows careful thought.

What could be more stupid and monotonous to draw than the mass of furniture in the third example. I think the background might with advantage have had less work in it; Brennan would have rendered every one of the details much more cleverly. But Jeanniot has made an interesting picture as a whole, breaking up one really inartistic line by another, and with the most unpromising details producing the best results. It is in artistically rendering furniture, bric-à-brac, and even old shoes, that men like Jacquemart have made their reputation as etchers. The same effects can be rendered quite as well in pen and ink, and stupid trade catalogues could be made interesting and worthy of preservation instead of being, as they are now, only fit to be thrown away as a nuisance.   Business men are beginning to understand that there is something in artistic advertising ; but it will take them some time to learn to pay for an artistically drawn advertisement.   I have been told that a large piano manufacturer in America has produced just such a catalogue, but I have not seen it.   With this drawing, those continually appearing in the *Century* and *Harper's* by Brennan, Drake, and Du Mond, and with the etchings and pen drawings by Jacquemart in his various books, there is no difficulty in finding good studies by good men.

Jeanniot has illustrated an almost endless succession of books and papers, *La Vie Moderne, La Revue Illustrée,* etc. etc.   The book by which his work has been made most widely known is, of course, the Dentu edition of *Tartarin de Tarascon,* which contains a vast number of pen drawings.

LOUIS LELOIR

THIS Leloir must not be confounded with Maurice Leloir, the illustrator of Sterne. The drawing here shown is a most refined rendering of character. The face has been drawn so well for reproduction that the printed result is more successful than any work I know of. And yet this is one of the very few drawings of Louis Leloir's that I have seen. Of course it is nothing more perhaps than a sketch for a picture, but when a man can make such a sketch he is a great master of pen drawing. The face and hands cannot be too thoroughly and carefully studied.

MAXIME LALANNE

To my mind, at least, Lalanne was one of the most exquisite and refined illustrators of architecture who ever lived. His ability to express a great

building, a vast town, or a delicate little landscape, has never been equalled, I think, by anybody but Whistler. To a certain extent he was mannered; so was Rembrandt; Whistler is the only man I know of who is not. The three little drawings which I have given show Lalanne's style very well. I do not know what was the size of the originals; in Havard's *Hollande* the illustrations are reproduced in many different sizes, but I think the small ones like those I give are the most successful. The student will find the book extremely useful.

Lalanne probably acquired his refinement of handling in the production of his innumerable delicate etchings. It is scarcely necessary to analyse his drawings here, as I have considered one of them in an earlier chapter, and all are characterised by the same sim-

plicity and refinement of expression, the same directness of execution. There is in them great knowledge of architecture, but this knowledge is not aggressive. The *Portfolio* contained many examples of Lalanne's work, among others sketches in Rouen and illustrations for Mr. Hamerton's *Paris*. His etching of Richmond and the Thames, which appeared in the *Portfolio*, is the most exquisite example of his work I have seen in any English periodical. Nearly the same results could be obtained with pen and ink.

However, the books which Lalanne illustrated are numberless. He did a great deal for Quantin, I believe. His work can be found in back numbers of

L'Art and nearly all the French magazines and periodicals, for he was a most prolific draughtsman. But perhaps the best, certainly the most complete, example of his work is Havard's *Hollande*. He was a very successful teacher, but because of the class of people who patronised him—principally royalties of more or less importance—this part of his life was wasted.

ULYSSE BUTIN

IT may be wondered why I give so much space to a drawing which is apparently crude and very like the projects and intentions of the old men. I give it simply to show the difference. The old work either is in pure outline, or if modelling is attempted, it is done in the most conventional manner. Here you have no outline, but, on the contrary, a masterly sketch in which the suggestion of modelling and the feeling for light and shade are remarkable for strength and character. Notice how the figure of the girl is suggested under her dress, and the simple yet excellent rendering of her hair, and the difference between her face and that of the man sleeping beside her. Of course this is rough work if you like, and the reproduction is probably about the size of the original drawing. But though the work is put in strongly and boldly, it is not done carelessly, and it is most interesting to see the way in which a man like Butin works. Note, too, that none of the lines are done with unnecessary coarseness in hopes that they will reduce into the proper relations with other light ones, but all are drawn apparently with a big quill pen. As I have said, I show this drawing more to mark the contrast between modern sketching of projects and intentions and old work of the same sort. It was published in *L'Art*.

PHO YVES & BARRET.

DRAWINGS OF SCULPTURE

IN looking over the catalogues of different art exhibitions, which are perhaps the only places where are to be found pen drawings of sculpture with any pretence to artistic rendering, one is struck by one of two facts. Either the sculptors have not made the drawings themselves, or else they have produced slight and trivial renderings of their own often very beautiful work. The chief cause for

this is that many sculptors out of France, singular as it may seem, cannot draw; that is, they cannot make a drawing of any artistic value. Of course in Paris this is not so often the case. A man who has gone through the *Beaux-Arts* is almost always able to draw. But in other countries it is the exception when the sculptor can. And again, it is extremely difficult to give with a pen, either with simple lines or complicated drawing, the real feeling of marble, terracotta, or bronze.

The consequence is that the majority of French sculptors, when they wish an artistic rendering in pen and ink of their work, not infrequently employ one of the three draughtsmen whose work I have here given to do it for them. Let us take the large drawing by St. Elme Gautier, after the high relief by Mercié, over one of the doorways of the Louvre. Mercié is a painter as well as a sculptor, his painting often being seen in the *Salon*, and he realises the difficulty of giving with pen and ink the effect of a newly-modelled relief which has none of the marks of time, or the interesting smudges and breaks and fractures which save the artist much work and lend charm to the results. But from new work you have to draw sharply and cleanly, depending upon nothing but your ability to draw correctly, taking the utmost care with every line, and yet avoiding that liny mechanical look which you will find at once in your drawing unless you are very skilful. One cannot call this drawing of Gautier's very artistic, but it is a clean, sharp rendering of the subject, and as such is a good study.

Contrast it for a moment with these heads of angels by Marie Weber. She has got all the modelling and the effect of the surfaces and the rendering of light and shade without a single outline, though Gautier's work is almost altogether outline. But a drawing like this could not be made unless the draughtsman was quite Gautier's equal. Notice how, though she indicates the lights and shades and the darks in the mouths, she has concentrated her blacks on the base on which the heads stand. And yet you will find little blacks all over the drawing, which is one of the most delightfully artistic renderings of sculpture I have ever seen. Other of Marie Weber's drawings are to be found in *L'Art*, but none that are as fine as this one.

Half-way between Gautier's and Marie Weber's work comes this drawing of Teucer by L. Gaucherel, which is an excellent combination of their two methods—of Gautier's firm bold outline in the light part of the figure, and of Weber's delicate modelling in the shadows. The effect has been obtained without a single pure black, just as, of course, there was no black in the figure itself.

Lastly, the head of De Lesseps by Ringel is an example of the work of a man who can model as well as he can draw, and draw as well as he can etch. Not only have his series of medallions of contemporary Frenchmen been most original in their conception and true in their execution, but the drawings are in no way inferior, and made a profound sensation a few years ago upon their

publication in *L'Art*. They are drawn on the *Papier Gillot*, and the cross-hatch, the double tone which increases the light, can be seen all over the side of the face, while the pure whites are obtained in the manner I have described in another chapter. It is, of course, quite possible that some of my critics will remark that this is not a pen drawing at all. I am quite well aware of this. There may not be a single pen line in it, though I think there is pen work in the hair. The darks are put in with a crayon. But as I wish to give an example of pen work on this tinted paper, even though it consists of only a few lines, and as this is one of the finest examples to be had, I think it best to give it, since I am sure it will be useful to students. By means of this tinted paper one can get nearer to the effect of a relief or an entire figure than can be done in any other way, except by wood-engraving, or by direct process from the relief or statue itself without the intervention of any engraver.

Among Americans, Blum, Wyatt Eaton, Kenyon Cox, and Brennan, by a process of his own, which I believe did not turn out very successfully, have made some interesting drawings of sculpture which may be seen in the *Century*. But by process or wood-blocks from the statue or relief itself a more telling result may be had, because sculpture depends not on lines but on surfaces, and by translation into line it loses enormously.

H. SCOTT

I DO not know if this artist is a Frenchman. But he lives in France, and his work always appears in French periodicals. I presume, therefore, he is one of the many Frenchmen of English or foreign parentage, among whom one at once recalls men, at anyrate with English names, like Alfred Stevens, Albert Lynch, and many another. However, nowadays the only artists living in a foreign country, who think it worth while to maintain and even assert their nationality, are Americans, owing to the duty of thirty-three per cent with which a beneficent government has seen fit to tax the works of art of all who are not fortunate enough to be citizens of my great and glorious country.

Scott has devoted himself to the picturesque rendering of architecture. He is not a master by any means, but he has done more of this work than any one else in France. Looking at his drawing, I should say most undoubtedly he was educated as an architect. In the headpiece, at Chantilly, the drawing of the flat mansard roof is absolutely expressionless and without character. It is impossible to tell whether it is of slate, shingle, or stone; I suppose it is slate, the material of which all French roofs are built. But there is no reason why a man should make a long series of parallel lines when a few, drawn with discretion, would have shown the material much more plainly. The drawing, or at least the reproduction, contains a great number of blacks, thus scattering his effects; but its chief merit is its expression of details which are very well rendered.

The large drawing is of course far more of a picture. The scraggy grape vine in the foreground is atrocious and meaningless.   But the light is excellently carried up the long street leading to the *chateau ;* the *chateau* itself is very well drawn, though there is but little light and shade in it, and some careless cross hatching on the towers.   The masses of trees are very wire-worky.   Taken altogether, however, as an impressive representation of a vast building dominating a small town, the effect is extremely well given.   He has shown everything, from the sally-port to the tops of the towers, from the great mansard-roofed *mairie* standing among trees on the left to the little working-men's cottages on the right, with great intelligence.   The roofs in all his buildings, save in the mansard of the *mairie*—and it might be better—neither represent light or shade nor their materials.   A simple reference to the Rico or Blum drawing will show what I mean.   The long straggling lines on the left of the *chateau*, though they lead into the wood and hillside beyond, are confusing. But with the exception of these details, and especially of the foliage, the mechanical treatment of which is to be avoided, I think the drawing an excellent model for study.   It is not given with the cleverness of Rico's work, an intelligent cleverness which very few draughtsmen may hope to attain.   But this style is one that can be acquired and is very well adapted to northern countries, as there is no attempt to render the brilliant glittering sunshine of the south.

MARS

MARS is evidently—I may use the term correctly in this case—a *nom de plume*. But here I care little for the draughtsman's personality, or sex either for that matter. I am not even sure if Mars is a man or a woman. But I am sure that as a caricaturist, rendering his drawings with an artistic feeling far beyond any mere artless or slovenly caricaturing, as an illustrator of fashion magazines, as a delineator of French *hig life*, or as one who produces charming children's books, Mars stands alone, and his work is recognisable anywhere. But there is frequently so much carelessness and so much caricature in his drawings, which are intended to be serious, that it is really difficult to find a good example of his work, though it appears every week in the French papers.

However, a drawing like this of *Pierrot blanc et Pierrette noir* shows the character of one side of his work—the only side I find worth considering seriously—as well as it could be shown. There is nothing remarkable about the drawing; it is most probably all *chic;* but it is filled with graceful lines, and is specially characteristic as an example of his delightful use of pure blacks and whites. It may look as if it were very simple to silhouette a figure in either pure black or white, but it is really very difficult to do it and still give any effect of roundness. It is this which Mars can do so well. Of course several of the Germans—Schlittgen and Marold—and Birch in America also draw in this way, but no one does it with the grace and charm of Mars. On one side it is only a step from his drawing to the German silhouette work, and on the other to the pure outline work of Caran d'Ache. Exactly the same criticism could be applied to Boutet de Monvel's drawings of children. But I do not think they are quite so simple or clever, and they are nearly always printed with a wash of colour, as indeed are many of Mars'.

A. LANÇON

LANÇON has often been called the Cat-Raphael. His drawing of cats was no doubt masterly. But in his pen drawings there is very little or no attempt to render the texture ot the fur; it is the modelling, the pose, the expression he has been trying for, and to me the work, especially the side view of a cat, looks as if it were drawn from a bronze of Barye's. This may have been the case. But what I wish to call special attention to is the fact that these drawings are made with the double-line pen of which I have spoken, and you will see all through them the three lines made at one stroke. Of this I speak at length in the Chapter on Materials. The two drawings are a practical example of the working of the double-line pen, and as such are here given rather than as examples of technique.

A. LALAUZE

I PUBLISH this little sketch of Lalauze to show that the clumsy lines without feeling or character, used so much by many English and American illustrators, can be avoided, and graceful sympathetic lines substituted for them. This want of grace of line tells greatly in pen drawing. The excuse for the liny line work of many illustrators is that it reproduces better, but I am sure Lalauze's and Louis Leloir's drawings prove the contrary. Even Maurice Leloir's Sterne drawings are to me unpleasantly liny; the lines are aggressive all through them. In this connection I must insist that only too often English and American photo-engravers are but mechanical middlemen, who in many cases do not pretend to do their own work, while, in others, they are so utterly ignorant of art they make no pretence to artistic reproduction. When the reproduction becomes in the least difficult, they assure you that it is quite impossible. The desire to produce really artistic work they do not understand. But I hope this book may serve to show most conclusively what may be done with process.

There is a considerable amount of chalk work in Lalauze's drawing. As I have not seen the original I cannot say whether the pen work was done over the chalk, the chalk being used for an outline sketch; but I think it more probable the chalk was worked in with the pen to remove the liny effect and to strengthen the pen-work.

Lalauze's etchings, especially his refined little illustrations in numberless books, are perfectly well known.

NOTE.—I have lately seen this drawing also attributed to Louis Leloir.

M. DE WYLIE

THE Wylie here represented I know nothing about, except that he has an English name and is mentioned in the *Salon* Catalogue as M. de Wylie.

His drawing of twilight is one of the most complete renderings in pen and ink of tone-work I have ever seen. Pen and ink, of course I maintain, is, like etching, the shorthand of art. But when a man can work out a drawing of this kind, and give the most difficult effect of twilight even with elaboration, there is no reason why he should not do so. This, however, is the only successful example of complete tonality in pen and ink that I know. The wire-work sky is very bad, and though the artist has given the right effect in it, the work is aggressive ; the means and not the result first strike your eye, and this in any case is wrong. But the masses of the trees and the distance could not be given better in any other medium. There is an enormous amount of work in the rich foreground, and in some of the deep shadows under the trees ; the solid masses of black are disposed with the greatest knowledge, and, unlike the sky, this part of the drawing does not show the means employed, and the lines are not aggressive. Had the sky been made twice as low in tone and the block hand-worked, it would have been better as a whole. But there is very little, if any, hand-work in the block.

The drawing is a wonderful example of the rendering of colour by black and white, and an especially good study of tree masses. It was published in *La Vie Moderne.* Some of Félix Buhot's drawings from pictures in *L'Art* approach, but I do not know any that equal it.

CARAN D'ACHE

CARAN D'ACHE, whose real name is Emmanuel Poirié, is to-day the most appreciated living caricaturist. His work contains all the essentials of caricature. His drawings amuse the whole world. No one but a blind man would refuse to laugh at them. They are composed of the simplest possible lines and these are arranged by a masterly technician. It is true the drawings are commonly printed with a flat colour wash, or else in silhouette, but he does not depend on this wash to hide imperfections of drawing. And in addition to its other qualities nearly all his work possesses that local colour, that quality of ridiculing notorieties to which the English caricaturist makes everything else subordinate, with the result that in English, or in fact Anglo-Saxon caricature, unless you happen to know the person or the subject caricatured, you can scarcely ever appreciate the humour. Take this drawing *Au Pesage;* I do not know who these judges, or weighers-in, or whatever they may be called in horsey terms, are, but I have no doubt, knowing as much of Caran D'Ache's work as I do, that each one is a portrait of some Parisian notoriety from Longchamps. For Caran D'Ache first came into public notice through the shadow pictures of the *Chat Noir*, every one of which had a double meaning of the strongest kind. These were silhouettes, and it is strange that silhouette work so well adapted to pen drawing has been used so little. Since then he has continued to produce either these silhouettes or caricatures in black or white or colour in the pages of *Figaro*, *L'Illustration*, and *La Revue Illustrée*, and he is now devoting himself more or less to illustrating books, among which are the *Comédie du Jour, Comédie de Notre Temps*, and *Les Courses dans L'Antiquité*, from which this drawing is taken. The whole idea is perfectly absurd ; the combination of the Parisians of to-day going to *Les Courses* and the Elgin marbles running a race is simply side-splitting, especially when it is worked out technically so well. There is no doubt that we outsiders miss half the point, but nobody can fail to roar while admiring the cleverness of *Station de Centaures de la Compagnie Générale ;* the *Heureux Père, Heurese Mère ; Il y a du tirage ; Mlle. Phryné ; Déjeuner du Favori ; L'Arrivée*, which is a masterpiece ; *La Mère des Gracches*, with all the little Gracchi in Cab, No. 1482 ; the arrangement of the De Lesseps family of which he never tires ; and *Le Mail du Prince Apollo*, where Apollo drives a four-in-hand, while the President Carnot, as Jupiter with the thunderbolts under

his arm, is trying to control the *Char de L'État*. The book is filled with this absurd combination of Greek art and modern French life, but it must be seen to be appreciated. It is published by Plon, Nourrit, and Co., who have been good enough to furnish me with the pen drawing—that is, the key-block over which the colour wash is placed.

I must refer every one to the *Figaro Illustré* for Christmas 1888. This holiday number contained what I think is Caran D'Ache's greatest work, *comment on fait un chef-d'œuvre*. But the publishers would not permit its being reproduced. I have endeavoured to obtain one of the series of drawings which have made Caran d'Ache's reputation, but this has been impossible—I mean one of the series like the Frost drawings, a style introduced, or at least popularised, by Oberländer. The omission, too, of work in this manner by Job Willette, Courboin, or a whole army of comic illustrators, may be noted; but I cannot help thinking that their reputation is owing more to their wit, their vulgarity, or their personality, than to the technical qualities of their drawings.

PEN DRAWING IN ENGLAND

PEN DRAWING IN ENGLAND

IN all the countries of which I have spoken, and in America too, the introduction of photo-engraving proved of the greatest advantage to the artist. It enabled him to work without considering a wood-engraver, who would have to pick out with the utmost difficulty and care, work which the artist did freely and sometimes in as many minutes as the engraver would require hours or even days to reproduce. But the pen drawings made by a brilliant band of young men for *Once a Week, Cornhill, Good Words*, the *Sunday Magazine*, and others — between about 1859 and 1865, degenerating towards 1875 — and for many books, especially the illustrated edition of Tennyson's *Poems*, the *Arabian Nights*, etc., were the best ever made in England. Nearly all, however, were drawn on the block and consequently lost. That the proprietors of *Once a Week* looked forward to the introduction of photo-engraving, and probably endeavoured to foster it, is shown by the numerous examples of mechanical processes which they published.

But in England, until French and American magazines proved the artistic value, and not merely the pecuniary advantage, of pen drawing for process reproduction, comparatively little attention was paid to it by draughtsmen. Even yet, but few publishers have discovered anything beyond the cheapness of the invention. There have been, of course, notable exceptions. The *Portfolio*, for which Brunet-Debaines and Lalanne did some of their best work years ago, has always, more or less, for its small cuts used photographic methods of reproduction, and usually pen drawings have been made for this purpose. The *Magazine of Art* has also begun to publish them within the last four or five years. But most of the English process reproductions have been until lately of inferior quality. The competition of the photo-engraver was directed towards cheapness rather than excellence; and artists could feel little satisfaction in the results of drawings reproduced in this way. For example, *Punch* preferred—and still prefers—wood-engravings, which cut so much out of the drawings, to process blocks, which ruined them altogether. But within the last few years several fairly good reproductive processes have been brought out here, and one photo-engraver, Mr. Chefdeville, a Frenchman, is doing work which can scarcely be surpassed anywhere. Many drawings are, however, still sent to Paris for reproduction; while, as a rule, English block printing does not begin to compare with French or American, and without good press work you cannot have good results.

It is unfortunate that in England few leading artists now draw with a pen. I have been repeatedly given to understand that this is because it is the tendency of the English school to think more of colour than of line; and so pen drawing seems with the many to be thought of no account except for a rapid unimportant sketch. If anything has to be done in a hurry, "Oh, make a pen sketch," is suggested. Naturally, this manner of regarding it has not been conducive to the progress of the art in England. There are probably still many English artists who agree with Mr. Hamerton in his belief that "one very great educational advantage of the photographic process is that the public, which formerly looked upon real sketches with indifference or contempt, as ill-drawn or unfinished things unworthy of its attention, is now much better able to understand the short-hand of drawing, and consequently is better prepared to set a just value on the pen sketches of the great masters." But it would be no great comfort or satisfaction to men of to-day to believe that drawings, on which they spend their lives, have no other merit than that of assisting the public to appreciate work, not so well done technically, by artists four or five hundred years ago,[1]—that pen drawings, the real masterpieces

[1] Of course, in saying this, I except Dürer and the other old men whose work I refer to elsewhere, work which I appreciate as much as any done to-day.

of Fortuny, Rico, and Menzel, are only helps to the understanding of the sketches of old masters. Work done in an old-masterly way by Sir Frederick Leighton, which can be seen in the South Kensington Museum on the original blocks, is quite as good technically as that of any old master. But in the so-called fac-simile woodcuts from these blocks the work is so cut to pieces that many are almost worthless for study.

When I speak of drawings made on the block, I cannot help touching on another subject with which I have nothing to do in this book, namely, drawing on wood with a pen or hard pencil for cutting. With the starting of the publication of *Once a Week*, about the year 1859, as I have said, the editors or publishers of that paper succeeded in drawing around them the most original draughtsmen who probably ever lived in England. On the cover of each number it was announced that its illustrators were Leech, Tenniel, Millais, H. K. Browne, C. Keene, Wolf, and others. The word others on this title-page hides the names of Fred Walker, G. J. Pinwell, A. Boyd Houghton, Luke Fildes, Henry Woods, H. S. Marks, Cecil Lawson, J. Mahoney, E. Griset, J. M. Lawless, Paul Gray, C. H. Bennett, Poynter, Holman Hunt, F. Madox Brown, Du Maurier, W. Small, and F. Sandys.[1] No paper, probably not even the *Vie Moderne*, ever had a more brilliant staff. Most of these artists, seeing their wash drawings utterly ruined by wood and steel engravers,—all the character being cut out of them, and the drawings themselves lost in the process, —drew on the wood blocks with pen or pencil, thus compelling the wood-engraver to follow their lines. Even with this method, so much was still cut out of the drawing, it is usually impossible to tell whether it was made with pen, pencil, or chalk. Therefore, while the drawings of the men of the *Vie Moderne* exist to-day, as well as their comparatively perfect reproductions in the pages of the paper, in *Once a Week* we have neither the drawings nor their fac-simile reproductions, but a translation according to the wood-engraver. The loss of British black and white work between the years 1850, and I should say about 1875, can never be replaced. Nor can it be too deeply deplored. I suppose what is left is better than nothing, but it certainly is not the original work.

The least known but perhaps the best pen draughtsman in Great

[1] For fuller description of this work see explanatory chapter on these men.

Britain to-day is George Reid of Edinburgh. He can, in a pen
drawing, give the whole character of northern landscape, so different
in every way from that of the country of the great southern pen
draughtsmen, while his portraits contain all the subtlety and refinement of a most elaborate etching by Rajon; in fact, he seems to think
Rajon and Armand-Durand the only men who can interpret him.
He not only understands the use of a pen, but apparently fears that
no process except photogravure or etching can reproduce his beautiful
and reverent work, a fear which at the present day I do not share
with him. Abbey's drawings are quite as delicate, if not so much
elaborated, and are well reproduced in *Harper's*, though their absolute
fineness is lost. It must not, however, be thought for a moment that
I mean to say any process for printing with type is equal to photogravure, which gives all the richness and delicacy of the drawing,
together with a softness and fulness of colour, not possessed by it.
It is to be regretted that Reid does not, by using process methods
and coming out in some of the larger magazines, take the place which
so justly belongs to him as one of the foremost pen draughtsmen
of the day.

An artist who easily stands at the head of his profession, as a
landscape pen draughtsman, in England is Alfred Parsons. He can
draw decorative designs of flowers with all the grace and beauty with
which Grinling Gibbons could carve them, and no higher praise can
be given. He will, with pen and ink, make a rosebud which one cares
to keep far more than a painting of the same subject by any other
Englishman; he will show a little valley farm down by the reeds in
the river, a group of trees on a hillside, or a wind-swept moor; and of
late he has begun to draw figures; while much of his work is so interwoven with Abbey's that at times you cannot tell one from the other.
Though Parsons' work is imitated even to his signature, there is no
one in England who can be named with him.

It is curious to note the inability of English artists to translate
their own work into pen and ink, or to do anything outside the sphere
of some one art. The surest proof of this assertion is that a few
years ago, when English art was adequately represented in *L'Art*,
instead of the artists, as in the case of many distinguished French
painters, making their own drawings, and thus giving their own ideas
and adding the value of originality to the reproduction of their

painting, they allowed a clever young Scotchman, Robert W. Macbeth, to do the work for them. He did it very well, and by this practice has made himself the best reproductive etcher in England.

How little good pen drawing there is in this country is shown in looking over Henry Blackburn's catalogues, in which it is the exception to find, from one end to the other, a pen sketch one would wish to preserve. It may be said that English painters do not care to give more than the merest rough notes of their pictures. But the truth is, to produce a pen drawing requires great technical skill only to be obtained after careful study and continuous practice. In England, and in the course of time the same thing will happen in America, a successful draughtsman as soon as he finds he can make, if not a greater reputation, certainly much more money by painting, gives up his drawing as if he were ashamed of it. The difference in this respect between the English artist and a Frenchman like Detaille needs no comment. Not only is the French artist willing to produce black and white work, but glad to do so. The same can be said of Menzel with his thousands of drawings, while Alfred Parsons and George Reid are exceptions in Great Britain.

Among the few breaks in the monotony of the long years of Mr. Blackburn's catalogues are the drawings by E. J. Gregory, one or two by Boughton, Colin Hunter, Herkomer, Charles Green, Sir J. D. Linton, Cecil Lawson, and some charming heads by Frank Holl. But the only drawings which really merit mention, as works of art in themselves, are those by T. Blake Wirgman, done after his own pictures. He has really cared, and he alone, and the result is his drawings stand out as by far the best that have been contributed to Mr. Blackburn's catalogues.

Hubert Herkomer is one of the very few men who have ever illustrated their catalogues with drawings which have a value of their own. His sketches of heads are full of character, strongly and simply put in, while his studies in the Bavarian Highlands, though greatly elaborated and almost too large for reproduction, are very successful.

Fred Walker made many pen drawings, but unfortunately scarcely any survive to be studied technically, having been drawn mostly on the block for the wood-engravers, like the work of so many of the other artists of *Once a Week*. One very charming example of his drawing can be seen on the wood at South Kensington Another, probably the best he ever did, which has not, so far as I know, been reproduced before, is in this book. He died before the days of successful process reproduction.

Some of Wyllie's drawings, notably those of the "Toil, Glitter and Grime of the Thames," published a few years ago in the *Magazine of Art*, are models for the drawing of boats and the suggestion of light and the movement of water. If Whistler would only give us some pen drawings like his etchings of thirty years ago, he would show himself to be as a pen draughtsman what he was then as an etcher of old houses—the greatest who ever lived. A process block from one of his first series of London etchings would be a perfect study for a pen drawing.

Walter Crane's beautiful decorative drawing, his book covers, his designs, his initials, his head and tail pieces, in pen and ink, entitle him to be ranked as the first English decorative draughtsman of the day; while Selwyn Image's work is quite as striking and original.

Although Du Maurier is probably the best known of the so-called comic draughtsmen, his genius to-day lies rather in his wit and humour and satire than in the technical excellence of his drawing. In the *Court and Society Review* for November 23, 1888 he calls himself a pictorial satirist, and this describes him perfectly. There is much for which we must thank the creator of Mrs. Ponsonby de Tomkyns, but at the same time it would be best for the student not to imitate his technique, since Du Maurier to-day, in his desire to express his ideas, seems to care little how he does it. He appeals far less to the art student than to the lover of satire. His drawings are a sort of sermon which happens to be drawn, instead of written with a pen. Every one, however, should study his work in *Once a Week* of nearly thirty years ago. I can easily understand the appreciative enthusiasm with which it was greeted by the critics of the last generation. It then contained all and a great deal more than is claimed for it to-day.

Harry Furniss is an extremely clever man; his drawings are full of character and style, and frequently his slightest sketches are the most interesting. His best work, I think, is found in his large drawings of the Essence of Parliament and in his small ones of the different members. Linley Sambourne's drawings also are intensely clever, but so near being mechanical that it would be impossible for any one to study from them without becoming wholly so. In his work, however, as in that of many another original man, the result is simply wonderful. Charles Keene's work in *Punch* is unfortunately nearly always engraved on wood and, before I had seen his original drawings, had he not written and told me that most of them were made with a pen, I never should have imagined it. The originals are among the best character drawings ever made in England. It is to be regretted that so much is lost in the cutting. Thirty years ago one could tell much more easily how his drawings were made; to-day it is absolutely impossible, a fact which is not very flattering to the art of woodcutting at the present time, as exemplified in the work of the engravers for *Punch*. Therefore, excellent as are Keene's drawings, it is useless for the student to study the reproductions in *Punch*, which give no idea of the original work.

As a matter of fact, some of the younger artists of *Judy* are the men on English comic papers who give most thought to style and technique. The drawings of Leslie Wilson and Maurice Griffen-hagen, who started out by working as much like Schlittgen as they could, are probably, technically, the best of all. Griffenhagen has since developed a style of his own which is very charming. The work of Partridge and Forestier of the *London News* is also full of character. Caton Woodville has made numerous pen drawings, but for the student I would suggest, rather than his work, that of Germans like Haug and Frenchmen like Jeanniot.

Cruikshank, Leech, and Phiz are responsible for the style, or rather want of style, of too many English draughtsmen. They had genius, but most of their followers have nothing but their weaknesses and imperfections of technique. The latter forget that the drawings of the artists they imitate were rarely done with the pen, and that if they were, it was only to be reproduced by engraving or etching on wood or steel, mostly by other men, and hence that the qualities of the pen work were cut out. It is a delight to turn from the English so-called comic papers to *Fliegende Blätter*, *La Vie Parisienne*, or the American *Life*, in which not only is there wit and humour, but a feeling for art not always to be found in English journals of the same class.

In the case of Sir John Gilbert, who has done much good work, freedom is the result of study. The same freedom, however, indulged in by a student would lead to meaningless blots and wild scrawlings, though all of Sir John Gilbert's blots and lines are put down with a purpose. A far better man to study would be Mulready, some of whose drawings are marvellous in their old-masterish feeling. A collection of them is to be seen at South Kensington. However, were Mulready and Wilkie living to-day, I believe they would utterly change their style. The attempt at so-called freedom, which on the part of the student is nothing but carelessness, is often sure to be his ruin. Look at the apparent freedom of a man like Forestier and then try to imitate it. Far better would it be for the student to follow the painstaking, careful lines of Tenniel in such work as *Alice in Wonderland*, for, though these drawings may have been made in line with a hard lead-pencil, and the student will probably not keep for long to Tenniel's methods, he will at least learn from them that pen drawing is not the easy slip-shod art he is pleased to think it.

The late Randolph Caldecott, separated from his humour and observation, shows very little technically to study. Unless a man has the genius to make in half a dozen lines a drawing like that of the mad dog or the cat waiting for a mouse, in which case he would be another Randolph Caldecott, it would be useless for him to study these drawings. Caldecott had enough genius to make him superior to technique. One can pardon his faults and ask for more of his delightful work because of his humour. I have recently seen drawings of dogs, cats, and children by Ernold Mason, which, technically, are far superior to anything Randolph Caldecott ever did.

It is just this pardoning that has such a bad influence on art, and has made men, who really technically never studied their profession, its leaders. The trouble is that because artists have good ideas, the fact that they cannot express them technically is overlooked. No ideas can be expressed in a really artistic manner without technique, which is nothing more than the grammar of art.

Hugh Thomson, a very young man, who draws figure subjects; Herbert Railton, who is very clever and draws architecture; and Gordon Browne, whose Fairy Tales were excellent, and who seems to have the facility of Doré, are three men who have devoted themselves almost exclusively to pen drawing. But one cannot help being conscious that it is the demand for photographic draughtsmen, rather than the real feeling for line, which has sent them to pen drawing. Hugh Thomson's best work is his decoration, some of which is very effective. Herbert Railton, having been educated as an architect, has probably better knowledge of architectural construction than any other draughtsman. But one finds in his drawing, as in all architectural sketching, a confusion between architectural and artistic lines. His drawings have not the effect of being made from nature, though they may be, while his architectural training asserts itself everywhere. This is less Railton's fault than that of the English system of architectural drawing.

G. P. Jacomb-Hood has made some notable drawings for *In his Name*, and beautiful decorative head and tail pieces for Mr. Lang's translation of *Aucassin and Nicolette*. Frederick Barnard also has done some very clever pen drawings, but he seems to have preferred, until lately, when he has come out strongly in *Harper's*, other mediums for his black and white work.

Finally, in summing up, I think that the examples in this book will show most conclusively that, with the exception of Parsons, Reid, Walter Crane, Griffenhagen, Forestier, Partridge, and Charles Keene to-day, the artists of the Continent and of America have paid more attention to, and have been more successful in, pen drawing for process reproduction than artists in England.

PEN DRAWING IN ENGLAND

ILLUSTRATIONS

INTRODUCTION

FOR the publication of pen drawings made some thirty years ago, I feel that an explanation is needed. While pen drawing, owing to photography, has advanced in all other countries, there is no doubt that in England its greatest period was just before photographic reproduction was invented. Very good work was being done all over the world at the same time. Meissonier, for example, was illustrating in France. But not only has he given up illustration, but his methods have been improved upon by the men who have followed him. In Germany, though Menzel still retains his position as an illustrator, he has always worked in a style well adapted to reproduction. In Italy and Spain at this period, no one was doing pen work of any special importance. But the Englishmen who illustrated *Once a Week*, *The Cornhill*, *Good Words*, the *Sunday* and *Shilling Magazines*, and the early numbers of *The Graphic* and *Punch*, have had, even in these days of development both in woodcutting and in process, no worthy successors working for English periodicals. The consequence is that I am obliged to show drawings by these men or else to ignore the best period of English work.

In some cases I have found that the original drawings were preserved or photographed through the interest the engravers took in their work, and also because, realising the uncertainties of woodcutting, they feared the drawing might be spoiled and no record of it left. The case of the Dalziel Bible is different. Messrs. Dalziel commissioned all of the rising young artists to produce a series of drawings. But the work turned in was difficult to do full justice to on the wood block ; Messrs. Cassell about the same time brought out their Doré Bible, and it was almost impossible for any one to rival Doré's popularity and productiveness. The consequence was that Messrs. Dalziel, looking ahead and seeing that photography would be used to transfer drawings to the block for cutting, finished a certain number and put the others aside for twenty years, and their Bible Gallery did not appear until 1880, when the drawings were photographed on to the block and cut, the original work thus remaining untouched. And now, nine years later, I have the admission from Messrs. Dalziel that they themselves consider the process reproductions I now publish from these drawings much more satisfactory than their own woodcuts. This, in connection with the fact that Mr. W. J. Linton is devoting the ripest years of his life to reproducing the masterpieces of wood-engraving, not by new woodcuts, but by process plates, is the strongest proof that I, at any rate, desire, not that woodcutting is a failure, but that it is a waste of time, labour, and skill, provided the drawing is made with as much attention to the requirements of process as the old men devoted to the requirements of wood-cutting, for a skilled craftsman to compete with a mechanical yet accurate invention.

Among the men whose work I have not shown, but whom I should like to have had represented is, to begin with, Rossetti. When I said in the Introduction that I wished Rossetti had not elaborated with pen or pencil in his drawings, I referred more especially to the drawings from his paintings which have been photographed and published in rather large size. For technically these do not compare for a minute with his illustrations of Tennyson, particularly those in the *Palace of Art*, drawn on the block and cut to pieces. Mr. William Michael Rossetti kindly offered to lend me a set of negatives which were rather generally thought to have been made from the drawings on the wood before they were cut, as in the case of the Sandys drawing. But the slightest examination of the photographs shows them to have been made merely from preparatory studies before the drawings were put on the wood, and their publication would be most unfair to Rossetti. Nor would it be fair to show as an example of his work the illustrations in the *Prince's Progress* and the frontispiece to the *Early Italian Poets*, which give no idea of its exquisite refinement. The only drawing I know of which may have been made for engraving is the portrait of his wife, which was never cut, and can be seen at South Kensington. Therefore I have not shown any Rossettis, except the one small cut in "Some Comparative Heads." He can hardly be considered an illustrator, though he did make so marvellous a success in the Tennyson. But even in it, there is but one drawing—the first illustration to the *Palace of Art* engraved by Messrs. Dalziel—really worthy of the extravagant praise lavished upon it; and as I have a beautiful Sandys, which is the work of an illustrator and technically even better, and as it is impossible to obtain anything but the wood block of the Rossetti, I have not considered it worth while to put it here. Moreover it would be the greatest waste of time to draw in such a manner and on such a scale in these days of process. That Rossetti and Dalziel did produce their result calls for all praise; a repetition of it would be laborious and misplaced affectation.

The work of other men in the pages of the magazines I have referred to was engraved by Messrs. Swain and Dalziel, I doubt not with the greatest possible fidelity for line, but the actual quality of the line, that is the quality given by pencil, brush, or pen, is in nearly every case lost. Therefore, though these magazines and *The Cornhill* and *Good Words'* collections of proofs should be seen and known by all students, it is really useless to publish any of the blocks as examples of pen drawing. But as cuts, the series of Parables by Sir J. E. Millais, especially the Good Samaritan, published in *Good Words*, April 1863, and the Lost Piece of Silver, in September of the same year, are enough to make any man's reputation. One of these men who, to my mind, is much less well known than he deserves to be, is J. Mahoney, whose drawings in the *Sunday Magazine* for November 1, 1867, and March 1, 1868, are, even as wood-cuts, equal to anything Alfred Parsons has ever done, and Parsons is the only man who can for a minute be compared with him ; the engravings by Whymper from Mahoney's drawings in *Scrambles among the High Alps* should also be seen. Of the rest, there are J. D. Watson with his great delicacy ; Fred Walker's *Adventures of Philip* and *Denis Duval* in *The Cornhill ;* Gordon Thomson ; J. W. M'Ralston's illustrations to Mrs. Craik's novels ; Sir Frederick Leighton's *Romola ;* T. Morten, who was good yet sketchy ; R. Barnes, Saul Solomon ; Basil Bradley ; A. Murch ; while the work of Pinwell, Sir James D. Linton, and the later men is to be found in the early volumes of *The Graphic*. Dickens was a magnificent field for Charles Green, Fred Barnard, and others.

It would be most interesting to publish examples of all this work ; but as it was not done for process, even if the original drawings could have been obtained, in many cases they could not have been rendered satisfactorily by photo-engraving, not through any fault of the process but because the artists worked without knowledge of it, while the reproductions of the cuts themselves would only prove the possibilities of process for reproducing woodcuts, and nothing about the drawings. Therefore, interesting as it would be, and difficult as it is for me to resist showing them, to do so is not within the limits of this book.

FREDERICK SANDYS

I HAVE been told that it must not be supposed Frederick Sandys revived illustration in the manner of the Germans of the fifteenth and sixteenth centuries, but that this revival, on the contrary, was due to the Pre-Raphaelites, and more especially to Saul Solomon, all of whom were themselves influenced by Menzel. But however this may be, there is no doubt that Sandys surpassed in technique all the artists of the best period of English draughtsmanship. His designs may not have possessed from their subjects that elevation of ideas which was so markedly the characteristic of the Germans, and which was the outcome of the spirit of their age. But there is no question that technically many parts of this drawing are quite equal to Dürer's work; while the modelling of the faces, the legs of the man, and the gown of the woman are drawn in a manner absolutely unknown to Dürer. There is a feeling of colour throughout which Dürer never attempted on the wood, because he knew it could not be retained in the cutting.

I admit that the photogravure in certain particulars is not as satisfactory as the woodcut of the same drawing by Swain, because it was made from an old negative taken from the drawing on the block. It shows the colour of the block, which Sandys never intended, and, owing to this or to the ink not having been uniformly black or having run, the lines are blurred to a certain extent. The negative too has faded, and many of the lines of the undergrowth about the middle of the right side of the drawing were apparently confused in the drawing, though they were corrected when cut. But I publish the plate because, with all these imperfections, I am not afraid to have it compared with the wood block in the *Shilling Magazine* for 1865. The wood block shows the drawing in the manner in which Sandys and Swain wished it to appear; the plate shows it exactly as it was drawn on the block. Had the drawing been made on a piece of white paper, and could I have obtained that white paper, the result would have been perfect, because no one has ever drawn better for process than Sandys. I do not say that it would have been an improvement on the woodcut, but it would have been reproduced autographically with infinitely less labour, and would have given Sandys' actual lines without the intervention of another hand.

FORD MADOX BROWN

IF this is Pre-Raphaelite work it is excellent. It is carried out with the careful reverence for line which is so characteristic, not of the men before Raphael's time, but of the Germans of Dürer's age, though without slavish imitation of any one. Not only is every detail, save the very funny chicken in the foreground, well drawn, but the feeling for the various substances and the differing texture of the garments is well given. Contrast the heavy robe of the Prophet with the lighter stuff of the widow's cloak and the grave clothes of the boy ; note the difference, although the tone is very nearly the same, between the Prophet's robe, the steps, the shadow, and the widow's gown, and the delightful difference of handling in each. Every part is worked out with the feeling not only for light and shade, but for line. In fact, one can see that Madox Brown took the greatest interest in the making of this drawing, in rendering a subject of the past with the technical knowledge of the present—the true and right spirit in which all art work should be produced.

Though for my own purpose I should prefer the cleverness of a man like Fabrès, a cleverness which is amazing and which in a southern subject I would unquestionably follow, to the student I would recommend this drawing quite as highly as the one by Fabrès. However, I must say that I do not think the effects of strong light, which exist in the East, have been rendered by Madox Brown so truly as by Fabrès in Italy. This probably comes from the fact that Fabrès worked from nature, Madox Brown in the studio. But the delicate suggestion of bits of light telling against the dark on the steps, the wooden stand relieved against the stairs, the relief of the heads against the white walls, and the delightful way in which the shadow of the little bird flying to its brick nest is studied, make the drawing equal to the work of Rico or any of the Spaniards and Italians ; though it is not so realistic, it is worked out far more thoroughly than any of their drawings, and in it the peculiarly English artistic idea of telling a whole story is expressed, not in an aggressive, but in the right spirit. Notice how the light from the lamp in the little upper chamber is carried down the light side of the post to which the rope that serves as banister is attached, down the rope itself, on by the widow's gown into the most carefully-studied interior of the living room. The contrast between the delicate face of the child, the severe head of the Prophet, and the agonised expression of the widow is completely rendered. In fact the subject could not be treated in a more satisfactory manner in any other medium.

By publishing these three illustrations from Dalziel's Bible, I hope I may show, not only my appreciation of them, but that the methods of thirty years ago were sometimes adapted to the requirements of to-day. There are certain details of line which will not reproduce, but I believe Madox Brown would have changed them had he known what was wanted.

E. J. POYNTER

THIS drawing of Daniel's Prayer for Dalziel's Bible is one of the three blocks made from the original drawings which I have been able to show. The drawing differs from Sir Frederick Leighton's and that of Ford Madox Brown in being carried out in the most complete manner all over, and in resembling in the handling a clean wiped print from an etched plate. Had I made a copper plate from this drawing and printed it with retroussage, I do not believe that any one could have told it from an etching. The drawing of Daniel and the figure in the background are excellent, and the careful way in which the detail has been all worked out is something remarkable. The result is extremely good; it is indeed by far better than any pen drawing made before Menzel's time, for of course to Menzel this style of drawing is entirely due, and Mr. Dalziel has told me he bought copies of Menzel's drawings and gave them to the artists who were then at work on his Bible. But, though this drawing of Poynter's is a wonderful example of careful honest work, I cannot conscientiously say that its style is a good one for a student to follow. The same effect could have been produced in wash with one-tenth the time and labour.

But as I have elsewhere said, this was the commencement of the reaction against translative wood-engraving. These lines of course had to be followed by the engraver, and when it is remembered for a moment that the engraver had to cut the whites out between these lines, some estimation of the difficulty of the task can be formed. And when it is considered that the process block from the original drawing from which this impression is printed was made automatically, I think it shows most conclusively what strides mechanical reproduction is making. As to the reproduction itself, the lines nearly all over have thickened appreciably, and in some places they have filled up, because the drawing was made on yellowish-toned paper and in parts in a very grey ink, and having been made nineteen years ago, it has also probably faded to a certain extent. I think a French, and I am quite sure an American process block from the same drawing would have given these grey lines, which in a few places have been entirely omitted, and in other places have thickened perceptibly or become rotten. But the principal thing I want to show is that it is possible to reproduce a drawing like this simply and easily by process, giving the character and feeling of the work, which this block certainly does; while the engraving of it on wood, line for line, is an almost impossible task with really no better results. For, as I have shown, in the woodcut you do not have the lines but the effect produced by cutting round them; in the process block you have the lines themselves reproduced just as they were drawn.

SIR FREDERICK LEIGHTON

I⊤ may be a surprise to many to find Sir Frederick Leighton included among pen draughtsmen, and I have no doubt I shall be told that this is not a pen but a brush drawing. But when a man makes a drawing as notable,—technically so remarkable,—conveying such an idea of strength and size and power, and showing conclusively what may be done with a brush used as a pen, it ought to be known. I publish it as an example, not of style for reproduction, but of the successful use of means which one would not think were fitted to the desired end. The whole effect could have been rendered, not with the point of a half-dry brush as it has been, but by splatter work and a pen. I would not recommend any one to attempt to imitate it, because, except by photogravure, it cannot be autographically reproduced; and though the forms and modelling have here been obtained, they could have been much more easily rendered with a wash.

Though the effect of the drawing has been reproduced almost perfectly, the lines in the hand to the right and in the leg have thickened appreciably, and it has darkened all over. The photogravure, however, is much better than the woodcut, which may be seen in Dalziel's Bible Gallery. The woodcut was a failure; the photogravure is an undoubted success.

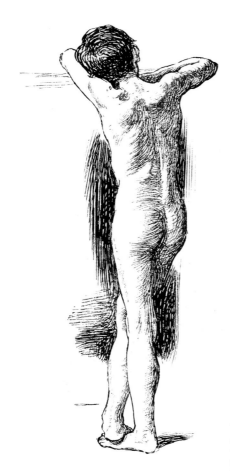

WILLIAM SMALL

I PUBLISH these four drawings as examples of good careful sketching of the figure in pen and ink, not by any means an easy performance. They have not been very well reproduced, but owing to the greyness of the ink, it has proved impossible for the photo-engravers to obtain the true value of the lines. I publish them also because Small's work, so far as I know, is always cut on wood, and I thought these little figures would be an interesting contrast to his best known drawing, and also to the work of Butin and of the old men.

W. L. WYLLIE

WHEN one considers the extreme picturesqueness of river life, especially of life on a river like the Thames, it is very remarkable that pen draughtsmen have not turned it to more profitable account. On the Thames, however, the reason for this neglect may be because Wyllie has made it so completely his own. This drawing done largely, freely, and boldly, mainly with a quill pen, shows, not only his command of the pen, but his knowledge of the construction of boats, the movement and swing of the water and the effect of sunlight shining through the bright but misty and smoky atmosphere of the river. The quill and brush have both been used. Where the roulette work is seen, it indicates his greyish brush-marks.

T. BLAKE WIRGMAN

I show two drawings by Blake Wirgman which differ both in style and subject, but are alike in their mastery of method. The portrait of Mrs. Smeaton after Reynolds, though apparently knocked off, is full of knowing suggestion of the modelling and colour of the original. In the other, of Mr. Armstead, he has expressed himself by line. Dantan in his drawing of a similar subject shows colour, Wirgman uses almost pure line, by which, however, he gets the modelling and suggestion of colour and indicates the surfaces. He makes the fewest lines tell with the greatest effect. This drawing and others of English sculptors, engraved on wood and much reduced, appeared in the *Century* some few years ago.

FREDERICK WALKER

WALKER is considered by the older men of to-day to be one of the greatest illustrators who ever lived. His subjects were always interesting, his sentiment popular, and his drawing exceedingly graceful. But owing to the fact that he worked before process, as well as to the methods employed by English wood-cutters, he was limited in certain ways in using the pen. For this very reason the results he did obtain are the more surprising.

The sentiment in his pictures is very charming, but in this drawing, as in so many others, it is neither true nor real. The colour and line and composition are most admirable, but in his time such a drawing could not be reproduced, and even to-day it cannot be well reproduced except by photogravure. This plate is the first fairly successful reproduction which has been made from the drawing, one on which Fred Walker, I think, would have liked to base his reputation; at any rate it was done in exactly the way he liked to work. At the time it was made, however, it was absolutely impossible to do anything with it. The consequence was it had to be redrawn in a much more open and much more mechanical manner for engraving, and the result can be seen in one of the early numbers of *L'Art*.

The English engraver of Fred Walker's time seems to have endeavoured to compel him and Pinwell and Keene and Du Maurier and their fellow-draughtsmen, even when they were at the height of their success, to draw lines which he, the engraver, could cut in the easiest manner. The consequence is that it is impossible to tell whether many of the drawings were done with a pen, a pencil, or a brush. I know it will at once be said that most of them were not done with a pen at all but with a brush, that is with the sensitive point of a very fine brush such as the Japanese use. They were also worked on with a lead-pencil and a pen, but in the engraved result, in the majority of cases, you cannot tell which line was made with a pen, which with a brush, which with a pencil; and I say that such a subjection of the artist to the engraver is utterly wrong. It is not that the wood-engraver could not cut almost every line that Fred Walker ever drew, but the fact is that he did not engrave it so as to show the actual means used to produce it. Wood-engraving can do almost everything, and even this drawing of Fred Walker's could be engraved on wood. But when we have a mechanical process like photogravure which will produce,

in as many hours as the wood-engraver would have to take days, an equally artistic and true result, there is no reason why we should not use it. This is one of the cases where science has rightly come to the aid of art. It is all very well for certain artists, who are not illustrators, to say that another man can render your work better than a machine; in a line drawing, in which you do not want any one's ideas or feelings but your own, no man can equal, though he may very materially aid, an accurate machine in its reproduction.

Though the idea, the composition, and the lines in the drawings of the men of Fred Walker's day are all most charming, and though the artists themselves considered the engraved results on the wood obtained from them most admirable, any one who will take the trouble to compare these engravings with the fac-simile engravings, or rather woodcuts, after Menzel, or with the work of some of the American engravers like Whitney and Cole, or Frenchmen like Baude, or Englishmen like Paterson, will see they are not admirable at all, but give, instead of the actual quality of the artist's line, that which it was easiest to reproduce. The engravers may deny this, but the comparison I suggest will prove at once the truth of what I say. Though no one can think more highly than I do of the endless number of varied effects which Fred Walker obtained, I cannot help feeling to-day that many of these are utterly unsuited to pen work, that they could have been gotten with far more ease with a brush, and that the reason Fred Walker drew with a pen was not from any particular love of line but to make for, or give to, the engraver lines to follow. One method some of his fellow-draughtsmen very frequently used was to make the foreground, or the part they wished accentuated, with a pen or brush in line which the engraver followed, while the background, in which of course they only wanted flat tints, was done with wash which the engraver could cut as he chose. The advantage of working in this way was that, if they made a mistake on the wood, they simply went over it with wash on which they worked with Chinese white, and the engraver made what he wished out of it. A good example of their manner of working can be seen by looking over the reproductions from the *Graphic*, published in the *Universal Review* for September 1888; though I do not wish it to be thought that I can commend anything which has yet appeared in this *Review* as good original drawing, reproduction, or printing. But in the number I mention these drawings, very much reduced, are all brought together and are therefore more accessible than in the *Graphic*.

There is another matter to which attention can be most easily called here. In studying the handling in the clothes of the figures in almost any of these drawings, especially those by Fildes, William Small, Pinwell, Houghton, and to a certain extent Herkomer and Macbeth, you find that exactly the same line is used by all, and that this same line appears in Du Maurier's drawings to-day. Either these men became mannered in an exceedingly short space of time, or else the engravers compelled them to draw in this abominable, mechanical, cross-hatched manner. Of course this same touch can be found in Dürer and the old men. But it is not a fine quality in their drawings. It is the expression of a mechanical difficulty which they could not surmount and which it is foolish for us to follow, imitate, or commend to-day. And so also I believe the growth of this cross-hatch work, twenty or thirty years ago, which has been mistaken to be a good style by so many draughtsmen, was not at all the fault of the draughtsmen but of the wood-engravers. And the reason for the position which Fred Walker holds among these men is, not so much because his drawings were better than theirs, for I do not think they were, but because he was more independent and refused to draw in this mechanical manner, although even in his work you sometimes see it cropping up wherever the engraver could put it. It is really the independence of his style, and not the excellence of the style itself, which has given Fred Walker the place he holds—and this is the surest proof that if one wants to succeed in illustration, one has simply got to do something for one's self.

GEORGE DU MAURIER

WHEN I first saw the engravings after the drawings signed Du Maurier made twenty or thirty years ago for *Once a Week* and *Punch*, I understood at once the sensation their appearance created among artists and critics. This work, really unknown to us of the younger generation, is as original as any ever produced. This drawing was published in 1865, and I only chose it because it was one of the first which specially appealed to me when studying his work in *Punch*. I might have shown a hundred others just as delightful, but all different and now unrecognisable as the work of Du Maurier. And yet with these drawings, at times published in the same number or even on the opposite page, we find the Du Maurier of to-day who, I must confess, from an artistic standpoint, I am utterly unable to understand. In saying this, I refer to his use of a mechanical cross-hatch to express almost all sorts of surfaces and of one type of face, and to his conventional and mannered drawing of landscape. But it seems to me that in the beginning his mannerisms must have been imposed upon him by the engravers, though now they are to be found in all his drawings. Du Maurier did not commence as a comic draughtsman. There is no comic element, no humour in his early drawings, for that matter, nor in many of his later ones. But every artist would wonder at his technique, his expression, and the cleverness he put into the very inartistic dresses of the last generation. No effect seems to have been impossible to him. He has tried in his early drawings to render daylight and nightlight, and even to work in all sorts of styles. There is one set of drawings in *Punch* in which you find Du Maurier burlesquing the Pre-Raphaelite movement so seriously as to be almost Pre-Raphaelite himself. In the early days of *Punch* he was pre-eminently a technician. He cared hardly at all for the story he was telling, but he cared infinitely for the way in which he told it. He possessed what Mr. Kenyon Cox calls the executive talent ; and this talent, the talent of the technician, is, as he says, in its highest forms as rare as any other. Du Maurier possessed this technical power of showing the beauty in the most commonplace and really uninteresting subjects. It is almost impossible to analyse it. One has simply got to feel it for one's self in the delightful way in which the absolutely uninteresting folds of the woman's gown are worked out, in the suggestion of modelling in the man's trousers, and in the study of light and shade on the polished leather of the lounge.

His work of to-day can be reproduced perfectly by process without the least trouble, and I should imagine, from the look of the woodcuts in *Punch*, that the old work—a drawing like this, for example—would have come equally well, in fact much more truly than in the woodcut.

CHARLES KEENE

THERE are very few men in this world about whose work every one has a good word to say. But Charles Keene is and deserves to be one of the few. The technique of his drawing is always excellent, his subjects interesting or amusing, and he has always striven to improve on his own methods. There is no draughts-man in England who has reached such a high standard, maintained it, and continually tried to improve it. I am not even certain whether this is a pen drawing, for the pen quality has been entirely cut out of it. But I have seen so many exactly like it done with a pen that I think it probably is. At any rate it is an example of very good line-work, of the study of character in the two figures, the modelling of the ground, and the suggestion of distant landscape. There is absolutely no reason why I should have selected this particular drawing. Those which have appeared in *Punch* during the last few weeks are equally good, if not better; and indeed the last thirty years of *Punch* are a record of Keene's efforts to produce the best character sketching in the best possible manner. His methods are those of extreme simplicity and directness of work, thought in composition, attention to modelling, and care in arrangement. Owing to the fact that he uses grey ink, always drawing for the engraver, washes here and there, and introduces pencil work, no process save photogravure will give a better result than the woodcuts by Mr. Swain. Photo-engraving would of course reproduce his work, but it would not be any more true than the woodcut.

LINLEY SAMBOURNE

When I speak in the English Chapter of Sambourne's work being almost mechanical, I do not wish to say anything that Sambourne or any one else could object to, for I admire his drawings very much. But the peculiarity of his style is that the actual technique seems to be founded on mechanical drawing, that is on the sharp, clean cut lines of engineering or architectural work. As his drawings are always more or less conventional, and seldom,

Process Block by Dawson.

Engraved by Swain.

if ever, wholly realistic, this is perfectly allowable; and that he should get such remarkable results using such peculiar handling is all the more notable. On looking over his original drawings I find that a certain amount of this mechanical look is gotten by the engraver; for example, the angular lines surrounding eyes and mouths are enormously intensified, and while of course these lines do exist in the drawings themselves you do not feel them as you do in the reproductions. Sambourne, working almost always for and with Mr. Swain, knows the result he is going to obtain, but one of his drawings engraved by some one else would probably not have this excessive Sambourne look, which is the only thing I can call it. The process block of the water baby compared with the woodcut shows this at

once, though the actual changes in detail—in the reeds and the water, for
example—were put in by Sambourne on the wood before it was cut; but the
hardness in the dragon-fly's wings and the very wooden lines in the woodcut

are due to the engraver. The actual loss in the quality of the line is visible
all over; I can feel it everywhere. That the process block is really not vastly
superior to the woodcut in the pen quality is not owing to a defect in the
process, but entirely to the fact that the ink used in the original drawing was
weak and pale. Sambourne knew this perfectly well, for he offered to go over
the lines. But the comparison could not then have been made with fairness
to Mr. Swain. As it is, I find the process block the more pleasing of the two
reproductions.

Of Sambourne's composition, which is always good, the lower drawing on
this page from the *Water Babies* is an excellent example, while it also shows his

ability to express himself in a small space. His drawing of the lobster and the
small boy looking at it, from the same book, is a characteristic example of
another phase of his work—that is his combination of human figures and

animal forms, often very grotesque. This large lobster drawing was done in such poor ink it would not have come by process. Though Sambourne uses but one female type, there is much grace and beauty in it combined with fine decorative feeling. The pages of *Punch* are filled with such drawings. The tail-piece is a characteristic example. It would be almost useless for the student to copy his work because, owing to this conventional treatment, he would only obtain an exceedingly weak Sambourne.

His drawings, to use an illustrator's phrase, are sure to make a hole in the page. His effects are almost always novel and catch your eye and interest you, even though the subject is very local. This is as it should be, for if a drawing is done in an interesting manner the subject is of minor importance. But it is for the pleasing fantastic medley which he produces in an impossible book like the *Water Babies*, or in his social and political allegories in *Punch*, filled with good drawing, that Sambourne's work interests the whole world, whether the local subject is understood or not.

We are starving

Harry Furniss 1883

HARRY FURNISS

O all the artists of *Punch*, the only one who habitually attempts caricature is Harry Furniss. But in his large drawings, called for some unknown reason cartoons, there is shown, especially in the one he has sent me to represent his work, the absolute want of all the qualities which I have noted in those of Oberländer, Frost, and Caran D'Ache. For you must be an Englishman to appreciate it, and you must have been on the spot and thoroughly in the swing at the time the drawing was made to understand it, while the work of the German, American, and French caricaturists does not altogether depend upon time or nationality. Even the most delight-

ful drawing which I know Furniss ever to have produced, the burlesque of Pears' Soap, was unintelligible to any one who had not seen the advertisement. This drawing of Education's Frankenstein, interesting as it is, will really explain what I mean. It is not done for all the world, but for a small section of the British public. In Furniss' smaller drawings, two of which I also show, and in his Parliamentary sketches, there is much more cleverness of handling, while there is no doubt that they give the character of their subjects. They look as if models had been used for them, but they also depend in almost every case, no matter how well they are drawn, on something exceedingly local. The consequence is that although one appreciates Furniss' great talent, at the same time unless one is thoroughly in with his public one cannot see the point

of his drawings, which in themselves are not sufficiently amusing to make one laugh.

The large drawing could not be satisfactorily reproduced by process, neither could the small ones. Furniss was working in each case for the wood-engraver and therefore did not consider the quality of his ink and paper. I have tried process with the lower figure on this page, but the woodcuts are better because the ink was not good. Furniss does at times work for process, and then shows that he understands its limitations.

GEORGE REID

GEORGE REID's pen work contains all the subtleties and refinements of a most delicate etching. He is one of those exceptional draughtsmen who can combine breadth with delicacy, who can elaborate a drawing on a piece of paper scarcely larger than this plate,—for Reid's drawings are mostly done the same size as their reproductions,—and yet obtain valuable results without niggling. The great feature of his work is its wonderful delicacy, its suggestion of colour. Look how the collar tells white simply by means of the fine lines which surround it, for it is no lighter than other parts of the drawing. Of all the men whose work I have shown Reid is the only one who succeeds in obtaining such delicate effects and yet makes his drawings the size he wishes to have them printed. However, the enormous difficulty of doing so must be apparent to every one, and Reid rarely makes any more pen drawings. Those he has already given to the world, however, are sufficient to secure his reputation as a pen draughtsman.

He tells me that he makes a pencil drawing from nature, then from this works out an elaborate study in pen and ink of the proposed size of its reproduction. This of course accounts for his remarkable certainty in his drawings. I cannot conscientiously advise any one to follow his methods, however, because they are too difficult. But if you can draw in his manner and succeed as he does, there is absolutely no reason why you should not. He seems to have no trouble in getting his figures and landscapes just the way he wants them, for he draws landscapes as well as portraits, and with them has illustrated three or four books. It is true that some of Parsons' work is very little reduced, but Parsons does not strive for Reid's very delicate lines, many of which could not be reproduced perfectly except by photogravure; though with a little more breadth of drawing and strength of line, I believe Reid could obtain exactly the same effect more easily by reduction. Du Maurier's drawings also are very nearly the same size as their reproductions. But then, in comparison with Reid's drawings, there is no fine work in them. As I have mentioned elsewhere, the photo-engraver tells you your work must be reduced to get fineness; Reid's and Parsons' work is the most positive refutation of such statements. But if with process and reduction one can obtain these effects I see no objections to doing so. Certainly it is sensible to take advantage of every means at one's disposal. Turn to the Blum drawing for example; it was not very much larger than the

The Author

Héliogravure et imp. A. Durand_Paris.

plate given in this book, but it was made for a very much greater reduction. In it there is nothing like the elaborate work which Reid has put in his drawing, and yet the result is just as good. The only characteristic feature of Reid's drawing is that he gets almost the etched line ; but very nearly the same line will be found in Blum's work.

The truth is that, although you must do your work with good technical style and distinction, if you wish it to have any value—and I believe all the work shown here has this distinction—you may use any style or combination of styles. What you want is to get a good result by good means ; so long as you do get this result it makes little difference what your methods are, provided they are good.

WALTER CRANE

WALTER CRANE has furnished me with this design as a characteristic example of his illustrative work.   His manner of working is to make with lead-pencil or chalk a more or less elaborate study of his subject, with a great and very proper idea of its decorative motive, on a piece of paper of the proposed size of the final drawing.   He then makes a tracing from this and works it out in pen and ink.   The drawing was scarcely larger than the reproduction.   There is nothing gained by reducing his work ; in fact I think the nearer the original size it is reproduced the better it comes.

The feeling of long sweeping lines and the suggestion of modelling in the drawing are very fine.   But when we look at the lines of which the drawing is composed, and we compare them with the work of men whom Crane considers to be the ideal draughtsmen, we find that, in his reverence for them, he seeks to perpetuate even the defects and imperfections which, had they been able, they would have been the first to overcome.   These defects were really due to the undeveloped stage of engraving and printing, when there were endless mechanical difficulties which the woodcutter and the printer could not surmount.   But in the preservation of the defects of these early draughtsmen Crane seems to be quite as faithful as in his admiration of their perfections.   Again, when we compare his cross-hatching and shadow lines with the work either of the early Italians or of Dürer for example, we find that he does not work with the care for each individual line which characterised all their autographic drawing, that is, their etched work or their work engraved on steel, which, and not the wood-cutting, is equivalent to the pen drawing of to-day.   This can be most clearly seen in the woman's face or the shading of the man's back.   The general effect is quite right, but the student who followed the lines would most certainly come to grief.   Crane's decorative feeling is also very fine and he gives good colour effect:

He has repeatedly told me and seems to think that process cannot reproduce his work, though he finds this reproduction satisfactory.   Nothing could really be easier to reproduce by process than his drawings were it not that he uses a very poor ink, sometimes for his shadows, getting in the result, notably in the shadows on the armour which express the

modelling of the man's back, instead of the grey he wants, a black line, the true quality of which can only be obtained by the most minute, laborious, and careful hand-work, either in process or woodcutting, though this work could be avoided if he were to adopt either the line of Dürer or the style of the pen draughtsmen of to-day.   For example, Howard Pyle's work shows admirably what I mean. As it is, Crane's drawings cannot be reproduced without this elaborate and, I cannot help thinking, useless expenditure of time on the part of the wood-engraver or the photo-engraver.[1]

[1] For other work by Walter Crane, see Chapter on Decoration.

RANDOLPH CALDECOTT

I THINK there is probably no one who has been so unjustly treated, by having been given a place to which he had no claim, as Randolph Caldecott. I believe I am right in saying he wished to succeed as a painter, a sculptor, and perhaps as a serious illustrator. As a modeller he was a success. Some of his beautiful little low reliefs are not half so well known as they deserve to be. As a painter he was a complete failure. As a serious illustrator, he either servilely copied the men working about him, or else, as in many of his horses and other subjects, borrowed from Menzel without approaching him. His so-called character sketching in Italy and America was either characterless or caricature, and even the best of this work in *Breton Folk* is technically of no value to the student. But there is a side to his drawing which, though it has been almost altogether ignored, is really the only side to be considered by the student. This is his power of showing expression and action by a few lines, often by a single line of his brush used as a pen. There is no one in England who has ever equalled him in this respect, and I very much doubt if any one anywhere ever surpassed him. I do not see how it would be possible to give with fewer lines the intense expression of the cat stealthily approaching the mouse. But curiously enough, although there are several other cats in *The House that Jack Built*, there is not one which comes near it, unless perhaps I except the cat worried by the dog on page 15, in which, how-

ever, the dog is characterless, while the intense expression which characterises the cat I give is wanting in all the others.

Again, has anybody ever given such a delightful absurdity as this of the dog who, to gain some private ends, went mad and bit the man? It is the concentration of action and expression. Could anything be finer than the two dots for eyes which glitter with madness, or the aimless expression of the fore

paws and the undecided pose of the whole body ? You have not an idea in
which direction the dog will spring, but you are very sure you ought to get

out of the way. The coloured plate on the
opposite page is very good, but what could be
more inane than the absolutely vacant expression of the young man in the background ? The
whole arrangement is excellent, but there is no
reason why, when a man tries to elaborate a
drawing, he should put in the houses in so
careless and slovenly a manner. The big dog
too, on page 14, sitting among broken pots and
plates is good, but Caldecott simply could not
work out a foreground. When a man draws
plants and flowers and grass, I at once compare
him with Alfred Parsons ; if he cannot give
them so well as Parsons, it is useless for the
student to turn to his work.

These drawings of course were done with a brush used as a pen, in sepia
or some other liquid colour, a method which, as far as I can see, was merely a
fad. Unless the printing is in brown, as in the picture-books and *Æsop's Fables*,
it is impossible to give any idea of the work. It cannot be reproduced in its
proper value, and absolutely the only object in using this brown ink to-day
would be to make work for engravers and colour-printers like Messrs. Cooper
and Edmund Evans. The latter has reproduced, as far as I know, all the
colour-work of Caldecott, with whom his name has come to be very closely
associated. The work of Caran D'Ache is done with a pen in black ink, and
the flat colour washes, which he like Caldecott uses, are lithographed or pro-
cessed. The work is far simpler and the colours seem to keep in their right
places with a great deal more ease.

It would be almost impossible to give a better idea of bounding free motion
than in this stag from the Æsop, with
the whole of Scotland stretching away
behind him, though probably the lines
in the shadow were better in the original
drawing. Then look at the happy fox
after he has fooled the stork, and the
innocent young lamb, probably just before he entered on his discussion with
the wolf. Take this lamb especially ;
technically I cannot conceive of anything

more innocent and childlike ; it would be simply absurd to attempt to copy such
a drawing, and yet everything you want is in it. It shows Caldecott's marvellous

power in expressing a whole story in a few lines, technically worthless, in his hands perfect. But the minute he went beyond this expression in pure outline, only to be surpassed by the cleverness of handling of Caran D'Ache, he began to

fall off. Note the action and go of these Three Round Hats. The first figure and horse are good, the boy on a pony is indifferent, the third man and horse and the landscape are absolutely bad; for when he began to elaborate, Caldecott was not able to express with many lines what he could indicate with one. If a man can express so much in one line as he did, he is really great; no one can follow him. If you have the same ability, you can do the same thing; if you have not, your imitation is sure to be artless and valueless. I know it will be said that there are cases in which Caldecott drew figures and elaborated landscape well; perhaps there are, but they are the very rare exceptions, and even in these exceptions his work cannot be compared with that of a man like Charles Keene, for example. What I want to show is every man's best work, and what I have shown is, I think, Caldecott's.

MAURICE GRIFFENHAGEN

GRIFFENHAGEN's work ranks to-day, in my estimation, with that produced by Du Maurier twenty-five years ago, though it has not the same variety. Each of his drawings is made with the understanding of the possibilities of pen drawing which characterised Du Maurier's work and so justly made his reputation. Although Griffenhagen started in the manner of Schlittgen and the other Germans, he has developed a style and character of his own. The features of his work are his refinement and delicacy of line, and his suggestion of modelling, surfaces, and texture by single lines. He uses scarcely any cross-hatching, and therefore his drawings come well by process.

HUGH THOMSON, HERBERT RAILTON

HUGH THOMSON began, to a certain extent, by studying the imperfections of Caldecott. His horses were Caldecott's horses, his figures were caricatures of Caldecott's caricatures; and until lately he has always drawn the same horse and the same man. But I am able to show one of his most recent drawings in which he has got rid of a vast amount of these mannerisms, and has commenced to work in a style of his own. This drawing is as full of go and movement as anything in the book; he has probably taken his ideas from Remington, who, however, is a far better man to study for the purpose than Caldecott; but these ideas he has expressed entirely in his own way. If he continues to improve at this rate, there is no doubt that he will produce something far better than he has ever done. The grass in the foreground is over elaborated without being expressive, and the faces have very little character, though still much caricature;

but this can be overlooked because there are so many good qualities in the drawing, which is unquestionably the best of his I have yet seen.

I put Herbert Railton with Hugh Thomson because they have done so
much work together, especially in the *English Illustrated Magazine*.   It is true

Railton has his figures drawn by John Jellicoe, and I cannot but think it an
enormous mistake for him, or any one else, to depend upon others in this
manner.   The first time one sees Railton's work, one is struck with its bright-
ness, cleverness, and go.   Looking at this drawing alone, one is charmed by the
clever way in which he draws a plain wall, indicates a bulging old roof, and
throws in a bit of sky, and although it is at once seen that he has paid no atten-

tion to the light and shade or tone of the drawing, one is interested in studying the way he works.   But when one takes up drawings of Westminster Abbey, of all the post-roads of England, of the towns of Normandy, and of the walls of Nuremberg, and sees exactly the same touch; when one finds that all his windows open in the same manner and all his trees grow in the same fashion, one must regret that a man of his cleverness and ability either never draws directly from nature, or, if he does, seems to care so little for what is about him. His mannerisms give his drawings, at first very pretty, an endless monotony. He is apt to elaborate patches of meaningless shadow in the midst of his lights, to fill his reflections in water with spotty blacks, and to kill what might be fine effects by scattering these blacks all over the drawing.   But it is because he has such great ability that one cannot help criticising him, as one would not criticise a man less strong.   The best reproductions of Railton's drawings, all of which, however, come very well by process, are the photogravures in a late edition of Lamb's *Essays,* in which they are reduced so much that his mannerisms are lost sight of and the results are very pleasing.   It is to be regretted that the publishers call these etchings, in the endeavour to give them a commercial fictitious value.   That the critic calls them etchings is not surprising ; it would be surprising if he were able to distinguish between a photogravure and an etching.

LESLIE WILLSON AND
J. RAVEN HILL

WHENEVER a man endeavours in any way to produce something out of the common, he is deserving of praise. Both Leslie Willson and Raven Hill, seeking inspiration on the Continent, have infused some life and go and technique into English comic drawings, and have shown, in their publication *Pick-Me-Up*, that there is no necessity to overload a paper with politics in order to obtain comedy. The example by Willson proves that he has broadened, at least in this drawing, and cleared himself of the charge I made against him of only working after Schlittgen; save in the figure of the near woman there is little German feeling in it, while it has a large amount of character of its own, though one can see he has studied, as every draughtsman who wishes to get breadth and character into his drawing should, the methods of the best men on the Continent. I find suggestions of Myrbach and Mars, Rossi and Rochegrosse.

In the drawing by Raven Hill, clever as it is, for he has utilised the methods of Jean Béraud and Ludwig Marold, I do not find any English character at all. The flower-girls are characterless, and the hansom and lamp-post, which should give at once the stamp of London, are excessively careless. But the execution is brilliant and the concentration of blacks extremely good. I also want to call attention in this block to the dotted tint which may be seen in the overskirt of the girl to the left, on the ribbons of the girl in the foreground, and in the extreme background; it is very useful often to fill up unpleasant white spaces and to give the effect of a wash. The artist has either made a wash on his drawing or indicated that a wash should come within the boundaries of this dotted space; the photo-engraver places a dotted film over his negative or on the drawing and photographs the whole; the solid lines show through it, and the dots are also photographed on to the zinc plate or gelatine film from which the engraving is made. This has been greatly used by Courboin, Mars, and Adrien Marie in France; while drawing on dotted films or placing differently arranged dotted or lined films over the drawing was patented by Ben Day in America. But this method, unless very skilfully and cleverly employed as in Raven Hill's drawing, is apt to look mechanical, and I do not think it compares to the tinted ruled paper. However, it is needless to say that Vierge succeeded in using it without mechanical results.

There are several other Englishmen on *Pick-Me-Up*, among whom is Edgar W. Wilson, some of whose suggestive backgrounds, worked out in a Japanese decorative manner, are very pleasing and full of colour. The editor is also obtaining the work of such foreigners as Willette, Lunel, and Caran D'Ache, and by this method of procedure and his desire for the drawings of outsiders, I hope his paper may have the success it deserves.

ALFRED PARSONS

ALFRED PARSONS is a man who has transgressed almost every law of pen drawing. There is no shorthand about his work, there is no suggestion in line; but he has with a pen succeeded where every one else has failed. His pen work has the richness and fulness of colour and the delicacy of execution of an etching, combined with the most artistic elaboration that could be obtained with a colour medium. When a man can successfully carry pen drawing to this perfection of completeness, there is no reason why he should not, provided the result is, as with Parsons, artistic. With other men, however, it is usually laboured and over-worked.

HE manner in which he has arrived at this complete mastery of pen drawing is simply by regarding it as no less serious a medium than any other, by studying the light and shade in his subject as in the drawing at Long Marston, by seeking for tone and colour where other men only strive for line. Note the drawing of the distant trees, the curves of each leaf in the foreground plants in all the drawings, and the individuality which he puts into the stem and leaf and blossom of every plant he draws. His drawings of plant forms are also full of decorative feeling. He is a perfect combination of decorator and illustrator; if he gives you an eighteenth-century

initial, you may be sure it has been obtained from the best authority, just as you know, if you are a botanist, that his flowers are right. But work like Parsons' can only be produced by the most careful study from nature, and in no other fashion. As a general rule, I consider Rico's methods much better, and in a certain sense they are more difficult to follow, because Rico has the mind of a great analyst, and the analytical faculty is probably rarer than that of selection and complete rendering. But Parsons possesses this latter quality, as well as that of decoration, to a greater degree than any other man living, and the possession of such ability gives him a place apart. As to the drawings themselves, they are made on smooth Whatman paper with inks more or less diluted with water. Their great feature is not the cleverness with which they are done, but the truth with which every thing is drawn, and the marvellous manner in which difficulties hitherto considered insurmountable by pen draughtsmen have been conquered.

The photogravure from *She Stoops to Conquer*, reproduced by Amand-Durand, is the best example of decorative realism that I could possibly show. The shield and the lettering might be the work of a decorator of Goldsmith's day. But no one has ever made such exquisite studies of roses as those which surround and build up this most original title. The flowers grow and stretch across the design with all that feeling for curves and direction which the old men rendered by a single line. Parsons' work contains these lines, but they are hidden among the flowers, and each spray and each flower and each leaf is worked out in a manner unknown before our time.

She Stoops
to Conquer,
or,
The Mistakes
of a Night.
A Comedy.

PEN DRAWING IN AMERICA

PEN DRAWING IN AMERICA

IF Spain and Germany were the homes of pen drawing, then certainly America is its adopted country. There the art has been developed altogether within the last ten years, more especially within the last seven. At one time American artists imitated the good English pen drawing of some thirty years ago, much of which, as I have said, was executed for the wood-engraver, and was therefore only known to them in the form of woodcuts. But they ceased to do so as soon as they saw the work of the Continent, which they could study in fac-simile reproduction. The principal American illustrators of the day unquestionably owe much to their study and appreciation of continental draughtsmen. Whom they took as models depended much on where they studied. Many adopted, as have Americans studying any branch of art, what seemed best to them in each of the different schools. Hence, though like Englishmen we have no national art school comparable with the *Ecole des Beaux-Arts*, nor the standard which such a school supplies, Americans have on the other hand, what Englishmen have not, and, whether rightly or wrongly, do not seek to cultivate, an eclectic appreciation of good art whenever we see it, no matter where it comes from. Any one, who has been at all out of England, knows how really little good modern art of any foreign school is to be seen in this country.

One American has taken Menzel as his model; another Dietz and the artists of *Fliegende Blätter;* a whole school now worships Fortuny, Vierge, Rico, Casanova, and the other Spaniards, reverently but with judgment at the same time; while there are some artists who follow Detaille and De Neuville, intelligently adopting French methods to their own needs. These men have in turn many imitators who, however, are without knowledge of all the underlying principles of pen drawing. The principal credit for this development must be ascribed to the intelligent support which Mr. A. W. Drake, the art editor of the *Century*, then *Scribner's Monthly*, was the first to give to the group of young men who, about this time, returned from a course of several years' study in Munich with the idea of revolutionising art in America—then a not very wonderful thing to do—by converting it to the school of Munich, especially to the school of Dietz. Among the Munich men were William M. Chase, who made some strong figure studies, Walter Shirlaw, who gave some of the most artistic renderings of commonplace things ever produced in America, Frederick Dielman and Henry Muhrman. A little later Reginald Birch returned, and though he was heralded by less blowing of trumpets, he has sustained and improved the reputation he made with his first drawings. The last book he has illustrated, *Little Lord Fauntleroy*, is probably the best thing he has ever done. Every number of *St. Nicholas* is made more interesting by his work. The infection quickly spread to what was then Harper's brilliant shop, working in, or for which were such artists as Edwin A. Abbey, Charles S. Reinhart, Howard Pyle, A. B. Frost. The entire revolution was not altogether due to the Munich students. But certainly they, together with the Centennial Exhibition, showed to a vast number of Americans, among others to those artists who had never been abroad, what foreign standards of technique really were.

About the same time, or a little later, between 1877 and 1879, Alfred Brennan and Robert Blum began to be known. They commenced to study in Cincinnati to a certain extent under Frank Duveneck and H. F. Farny. The latter is in many ways one of the most original, if erratic, of American artists. He had then already produced some very good pen drawings published in the *Art Review*, and he has added to his reputation by his brilliant drawings of

Indians published in the *Century* and *Harper's*, and by his illustrations for school books, of which he has made something artistic. From Cincinnati, Blum and Brennan went to Philadelphia where, like many another student, they received everything but encouragement to continue in the way they had marked out for themselves. But they found a friend in Stephen J. Ferris, who then, though he did not own originals, had photogravures or reproductions of almost all the drawings of Fortuny, Rico, and Boldini; and through these he introduced them and his son, Gerome Ferris, as he later did me—and for this I can never be thankful enough to him—to an entirely new world. Ferris, Peter and Thomas Moran, J. D. Smillie, and several others, by reproducing the pen drawings and the pictures of the greatest men of the Continent for the art books issued by Gebbie and Barrie, probably did as much to make known the work of European pen draughtsmen to Americans as any one else. However, even in the present state of international copyright, it is not likely that any of these books will be seen in Europe.

Ferris was one of the first artists to practise etching on glass, as it was miscalled—that is, drawing on a sheet of glass coated with collodion, which had been exposed in a camera at a white wall and so turned a dark grey or brown colour, and then varnished; then on this plate a drawing was made with an etching needle, a pen or any sharp point, and the result was either reproduced by photo-lithography or printed in a photographic printing-press. It was work like this, done about ten or fifteen years ago, which had an enormous influence in developing photo-engraving. Mrs. Elinor Greatorex, in her illustrations of old New York, I believe used the same process. Another man who made many experiments in other ways was B. Day. Brennan, too, continually made discoveries in process work, in which he was aided by the *Century's* Art Department. But without the assistance of Mr. De Vinne, the printer of the *Century*—a man who has devoted his life to artistic printing and succeeded in it—comparatively little advance would have been made. A glance at the magazines of 1876 will prove this.

In New York, Blum and Brennan found instant recognition, and a place for their work both in a sort of memorial to Fortuny and in the *Century*, then *Scribner's*. Here they were joined by F. Lungren and Kenyon Cox. From that day to this their work has contributed to maintain the high position which the *Century* and *St. Nicholas* hold among illustrated magazines. Much has been said about their originality. But their real originality consists in their intelligent adaptation of the methods of Fortuny, Rico, and Vierge, of the artists of *Fliegende Blätter*, and of the draughtsmen of Japan, and in their production, under all these many and opposing influences, of vigorous and charming pictures of their own. Brennan most certainly was and is the master of this school of American pen draughtsmen.

In 1878, I think, Abbey, who was then illustrating Herrick's *Poems*, came to England, and a knowledge of the country and things he had long cared for started him on a brilliant career, and has carried him forward until he is now the greatest English speaking illustrator the world has ever seen. For grace and refinement he ranks second to no one. In England of the eighteenth century he is as much at home as Austin Dobson. He can reconstruct its old rooms and village streets and fill them anew with beauty and life. In his old furniture and bits of glass and silver ware he rivals in fidelity and execution De Neuville and Jacquemart. And all of his work is in a style that delights the purist. It is simple, honest, and straight-forward. So also is the drawing of Reinhart, who, about the same time as Abbey, came abroad again—he having studied before in Germany—and, finding his chance in illustrating a trip to Spain, began an equally brilliant career. His work is always devoted to the things of modern life. He puts Mr. Howells' characters on paper with just that last touch of realism which an illustrator can give better than the author; while he has only finished telling the world what he thinks about American sea-shore resorts and the people who go to them. His drawings of France and England, done boldly, directly, and vigorously, are life itself. Nothing better than the work of these two men could be found for Englishmen and Americans to study. One cannot but wish that Abbey too would give us a little more of what is happening about him, instead of occupying himself almost altogether with the people and things of other days. His editions of *She Stoops to Conquer* and Herrick's *Poems* have never been approached in modern times.

Howard Pyle has given in his pen drawings the quaintness of American life in the colonial period, and, in *Robin Hood*, some beautiful ideas of a country he does not know. His *Pepper and Salt* and other children's books are as beautiful in their old and quaint simplicity.

Harry Fenn has illustrated many books and magazines. He works apparently with equal facility in all sorts of mediums. If he would concentrate his power on something that he made distinctly his own, as he did with wash in *Picturesque America*, he would hold a very high place as a pen draughtsman. There is no one probably who has such perfect command of his materials, and who, though often doing work which cannot be interesting to him, is always sure of getting striking and, very often, novel and artistic results. His drawings of interiors are models of arrangement and knowledge of details, and very clever as a whole. His work, as well as its reproduction, has vastly improved since he made the illustrations for *Picturesque America*.

A. B. Frost and W. A. Rogers, who can be either funny or serious to good purpose, have produced some of the funniest drawings, which rival those of *Fliegende Blätter* in their technical work and humour—though very different; and, like them, are good because they are understandable in all languages, and need no label to explain them. Of caricatures, pure and simple, are to be mentioned those of Thomas Nast and M. A. Wolf, which, however, have no technical pretensions. The same can be said of those of Mat Morgan and a host of other caricaturists. J. D. Mitchell, S. W. Van Schaick, W. H. Hyde, C. J. Taylor, are other comic pen draughtsmen who really are clever. But to mention them all would be to make a catalogue. Among the older men, of course, we have Darley's lithographed outline illustrations to Washington Irving, which I suppose were done with a lithographic pen on stone; but, of course, he started and formed his ideas and settled his style long before the time of process. Among the painters is Mr. Wyatt Eaton, who produced the noble head of Lincoln, engraved by Cole, in the *Century*, and the drawings after Olin Warner, also published in the *Century;* while another man who has done a great deal of portrait work in the style of, though not equal to, Desmoulins, is Jacques Reitch.

The only men of any note who have appeared in the last two or three years are E. W. Kemble, whose delineations of old darkies and the wild west are very life-like, but often very careless; Frederick Remington, whose drawings of horses in action are wonderfully spirited ; and F. Childe Hassam, whose work has certainly a character of its own.

Miss Jessie M'Dermott and Miss Alice Barber both draw well, but have not illustrated other work, or done work of their own to sufficient extent, to be given the place they would otherwise hold. The same may be said of many other men and women—Thurlstrop, Graham, Zogbaum, Redwood, for example. But the great bulk of their work is not done in pen and ink, and they do not seem to care for it more than for other mediums. The drawings of the artists I have mentioned will live long after the present generation.

So much of Alfred Parsons' work is published in America that one has come to think of him as an American. But of his pen drawings I have already spoken. Frank L. Kirkpatrick makes excellent pen drawings, but painting almost altogether, one sees comparatively little pen work from him. And this is also to be said of F. S. Church, who is strikingly original in his treatment of birds and animals. L. S. Ipsen,—who, among other things, has recently published some charming decorations, though the figures are not good, for Mrs. Browning's *Poems*, — George Wharton Edwards, and H. L. Bridwell, have given a decorative character to many of the books and magazines of America, which places them second only to men like Habert-Dys. W. H. Drake and Otto Bacher render arms and armour and many unpicturesque subjects in an original manner ; while Hughson Hawley, F. Du Mond, and Camille Piton have devoted themselves to architecture.

In looking at pen drawing, or rather all illustrative work in America, outside of the *Harper, Century*, and *Scribner* publications, *Life* and *Wide Awake*, the process work in *Puck*, and a few of the art periodicals, it seems as if the art editors of the various illustrated papers were trying to see which one could fill his magazine or weekly with the worst and cheapest drawings. One cannot but fear that unless there is another reaction like that which followed the Centennial Exhibition, art in America will fall to a lower level than it has ever held before.

PEN DRAWING IN AMERICA

ILLUSTRATIONS

EDWIN A. ABBEY

THE fact that I have devoted more space to certain Spaniards, Frenchmen, and Germans, and less to some of the equally well-known and important Englishmen and Americans, deserves, I think, a word of explanation. Too many of Menzel's drawings could not be shown, nor could I give too many of Abbey's. But while it is the duty of every illustrator and every one who cares for illustration to see all the work which Abbey produces—and it can be seen in the pages of *Harper's Monthly*—and while every pen draughtsman should own the charming *Herrick*, the monumental *She Stoops to Conquer*, and the lovely *Old Songs*, which have been reproduced by the best modern mechanical and wood engravers and printed in the most careful manner, it is scarcely possible for any one to obtain the original editions of Menzel's work, and in many cases reproductions from these original editions or new editions have never been published. Of the *Uniforms of the Army of Frederick the Great* I know of only one easily accessible copy in England; this one is in the British Museum, but very likely there may be a few more. The case of Rico and Vierge is almost parallel; it is even more difficult to find the drawings of many of the principal Spaniards than those of Menzel.

Abbey began in the wood-engraving office of Van Ingen and Snyder in Philadelphia, and, like so many other illustrators, he learned the mechanical part of his work in the daytime and studied art at night, to a certain extent under Isaac L. Williams and in the Academy of Fine Arts. But he soon went to New York and entered the office of Messrs. Harper and Brothers, where he continued for several years, producing much work in many different mediums for all of Messrs. Harpers' periodicals. Though his early work was wanting in the grace and refinement which has now placed him in a position without a rival among English-speaking draughtsmen, it was always remarkable for its quiet humour and its suggestiveness, while his marvellous mastery of

technique was quickly attained. Although he has gained a knowledge of
composition, a largeness of feeling, and a completeness of expression with his
years of practice, some of the drawings in the *Herrick* are equal in many ways
to his later work. As a whole, however, his last book, the *Old Songs*, is
infinitely finer than anything he has yet done. His drawings have become so
refined that no engraving can reproduce every line in them. He has selected
the two girls on the sofa from *She Stoops to Conquer*, and it is interesting to

compare this reproduction, which is probably better than any made from his
work, with the block in the magazine and the plate in his book; I think it will
at once be seen that it contains more of the feeling of his drawing than either of
the others.

While the superficial qualities of Abbey's work can be imitated by any one,
his rendering of the seventeenth and eighteenth centuries, which he has recon-
structed so wonderfully, will never be approached on the lines he is following.
His present position as an illustrator has been attained and maintained simply
by treating illustration, as it should be treated, as seriously as any other branch
of art. He is remarkable not so much for academic correctness—as is Menzel,

for example—but rather for his truth, the beauty of his line and his power of expression. No illustrator has realised more beautiful women or finer swaggering gallants, and no one has placed them in more appropriate surroundings. He makes the figures real for us because all the backgrounds and accessories are taken directly from nature.

Any one can see for one's self how drawing like this is produced; a more or less rough pencil-sketch is made on a sheet of very thin smooth paper mounted on pasteboard, something like London board, and the completed subject, which he has in his mind before he touches the drawing, gradually grows out of the models he has before him, and nature to which he always refers; and this is the only way in which great illustration can be and should be produced. The book plate, the drawing for which Mr. Gosse was good enough to lend me, is one of those numberless designs Abbey is for ever making for his friends; other examples of these charming suggestive conceits may be found in the frontispiece of Mr. Ashby-Sterry's *Lazy Minstrel*, Mr. Austin Dobson's *Sign of the Lyre*, Miss Strettell's *Spanish and Italian Folk-Songs*, in many other books and catalogues of his friends' pictures. In the book plate for Mr. Gosse, the greys all over the drawing are utterly lost; no process or engraver could render them. But no matter how much is lost, a vast amount of beauty remains. It has already been very well engraved by Mr. J. D. Cooper, but the result is not better than, if as good as, Messrs. Dawson's photo-engraving. I suppose that one might criticise the drawing for the utter want of the old conventional decorative feeling, but when so much that is new and good can be found in it, I think one ought rather to rejoice for what we have obtained and not mourn over what has not been given.

NOTE.—After a rather careful examination of the drawings and engravings in the Paris Exhibition of this year (1889), I cannot help being conscious of the fact that I have not given Abbey the place which he really deserves. Menzel is the founder of modern illustration; Fortuny, Rico, and Vierge have been its most powerful apostles, and among the cleverest men their influence will never grow less. But while Menzel's methods are obsolete, and Vierge's style can only be attempted by the most brilliant, any one can see that a new school is arising, and this is the school of Abbey, who has at the present moment followers in every illustrating country in the world, men who are seeking to carry out his method of brilliant drawing carefully and seriously executed. And really on the same plane with him must be placed Alfred Parsons and Reinhart.

American pen drawing, this Exhibition conclusively proves, is the best, and American process reproduction is the most sympathetic, and American printing the most careful, and it is this harmonious co-operation which has enabled Abbey to become not only, as I have written, the greatest English-speaking illustrator, but the greatest living illustrator.

C. S. REINHART

IT would be a mere waste of time on my part to try to praise or even to criticise Reinhart at his best. He has been influenced both by Germans and Frenchmen, with whom he has studied and among whom he has lived for years. His drawings are notable for their simplicity, directness and freedom, often for their grace, and always for their character and expression. There is probably no one else who, with such simple means, could so well show the three American mothers in this drawing. He has concentrated his attention on the faces, but he has not been slovenly in the costumes, while his grouping is extremely pleasing. It is unnecessary to give more examples of a man whose work is so characteristic and well known, and should be studied by all who wish to produce good as well as realistic renderings of the life of to-day. His drawings for the last twenty years have been seen in *Harper's*, where he has shown his ability to work in all sorts of mediums. It is only of late he has in his black and white drawings used a pen to any great extent.

REGINALD B. BIRCH

BIRCH is one of those men who have studied abroad, and taken what they have learned to America. Not only does he know how to draw well, but he is familiar with the life of two continents. His drawings in the beginning were Americanised Schlittgens, but, while he is quite as clever as Schlittgen, he possesses, I think, more grace, combined with wider knowledge of character. In the concentration of blacks, the drawing of little Lord Fauntleroy carried off to bed might suggest Vierge, but the footman, the two housemaids, and the merest indication of the housekeeper's cap and one eye are thoroughly English, though the little lord himself is completely American. The other drawing is equally full of character, and the handling in these, as in all his work, shows the greatest amount of expression obtained with the simplest and most direct means. He scarcely ever uses models in his final work, but makes his drawings from studies, tracing these on to Bristol board which he thus keeps thoroughly clean ; consequently his work reproduces perfectly well.

H. F. FARNY

FARNY's drawing is an example of what is known among illustrators as splatter work, which I have described in the Chapter on Technical Suggestions. But it deserves a place far more because of its suggestion of colour and the strong character of the face; there is a figure, too, wrapped up in the blanket. The decorative manner in which the shield and bow are put in and balance each other is good, and in fact the whole drawing is very well put together. But, as I said before, I wish to call special attention to the way in which the splatter tint is managed. The figure, apparently, was drawn and then covered, probably with a piece of paper to protect it, and the splattering done all over it. Everything outside the frame of the background was then painted with Chinese white and the drawing continued on this ground when dry. The difference in the quality of the lines made on the two grounds can easily be seen in the reproduction, in which the Messrs. Dawson have been very successful in keeping this difference. But in their process they do not seem able to get very fine single lines, such as those in the lower part of the blanket which are rotten, though there is no rottenness in the drawing. The feeling of the drawing, however, has been very well retained.

HOWARD PYLE

A COMPARISON between this drawing, Walter Crane's, and the plate after Dürer will best show whether pen drawing has advanced. When I can print along with text a drawing by Howard Pyle, which contains many qualities Dürer could not have obtained save in an etching, and then never could have printed with type, it shows decided progress, not only in technique, but in the printing of an autographic reproduction of a pen drawing with type without the aid of a woodcutter, a process which of course was unknown to Dürer, but of which, had he known it, I have not the slightest doubt he would have availed himself to the fullest extent.

The most superficial comparison of Pyle's composition and handling with Dürer's will show what a careful student the nineteenth-century American is of the sixteenth-century German. I admit, with certain American critics whom I respect, that in some qualities it is very hard to tell where Dürer ends and Howard Pyle begins. In his *Otto of the Silver Hand*, for example, there are compositions which are almost entirely suggested by Dürer. But who has not made use of the suggestions of other men? That Pyle should do this in telling and illustrating a mediæval tale, merely proves his ability to saturate himself with the spirit of the age in which the scenes are laid, and to give his work the colour and character of the biggest man of that age. The entire figure of Time, in the drawing I show from the *Wonder Clock*, is Düreresque. But the figure of the small boy piping, although the lines of shadow are drawn in the manner of the old Germans, is not German at all, but nineteenth-century American, and this is true of the tree in blossom and the stony foreground. They are better than anything in Dürer, for the simple reason that we know more about landscape than the Germans of his time. This way of adapting the methods of an earlier generation to our own requirements is exactly what the old men did, and it is only by so doing art advances. Pyle has preserved all that was good in their work, and yet kept pace with modern technical and mechanical developments. I know his drawing is a frank imitation, while Walter Crane's is not, but I do not see where the latter has improved upon the old work. Every line in Pyle's drawing is as careful as any to be found in Dürer's, and this cannot always be said of Crane's. I have published two almost similar drawings and compared them, because unless one is able to see together drawings by two men who work for the same end by almost the same means, it is impossible to judge of their relative positions.

Among the books by Howard Pyle which every student should know, are *Robin Hood, Pepper and Salt, Otto of the Silver Hand*, and the *Wonder Clock*. Many of the drawings are wanting to a certain extent in local colour, a want only due to the fact that Pyle has, as far as I am aware, never visited Europe. But in technique they are far superior to anything that has been done in America, and, I hope it will not be too presumptuous for me to say, therefore to any modern work of this sort. They are carried out with a thoroughness and completeness which give them originality, even though they preserve all the feeling of the old work. They are almost equal as decoration to Abbey's and Parsons' realistic revivals, and would be quite equal to them did Pyle know Europe as well.

ARTHUR B. FROST, FREDERICK REMINGTON, E. W. KEMBLE

I GROUP these three men together, for not only is there great similarity in their methods of work, but they seem to me the most distinctly American illustrators we have. On the one hand, their work does not possess much of that intense brilliancy and cleverness which is so characteristic of the Spaniards; nor, on the other hand, has it any of the slovenliness which characterises so much English work of exactly the same sort.

In the three drawings you see that models have been used for all the figures, though Remington's has the photographic look which marks all his work. But, as I have said elsewhere, there is no reason why a man should not use photographs, if from them he can get good results.

The style of Frost's work is, I fancy, that which the men of Fred Walker's time would have used, had they been transported to an American town and taken enough interest in it to make a drawing of a subject like that of Frost's. Of course there is an exaggeration in all the figures; they are not so real as Remington's, but then Frost's indication of the men's clothes is much more true and carefully studied than Remington's, while Kemble, to a great extent, has ignored all details and only attempts the large mass and long folds of the women's simple garments. But in none of them is there any of that everlasting machine-made cross-hatch.

Each of these drawings gives to an American a characteristic rendering of country life: Frost's of the middle states or the northern part of the southern, Kemble's of the extreme south and Remington's of the far west. All will probably fall under the English critic's ban because they are not pretty or beautiful; but they are more than this, they are real, and genuine realism was the one quality lacking in the brilliant Englishmen of thirty years ago. In Frost's drawings I do not think there is a line which could be omitted or anything that could be changed to its advantage. In all three, the reserving of blacks is well managed. In Remington's there is a certain scrawl of meaningless lines over the grass which is found in nearly all his work; the drawing is not so well thought out as Frost's, and it has a mechanical look which is much more evident in this reproduction than ordinarily, because his drawings

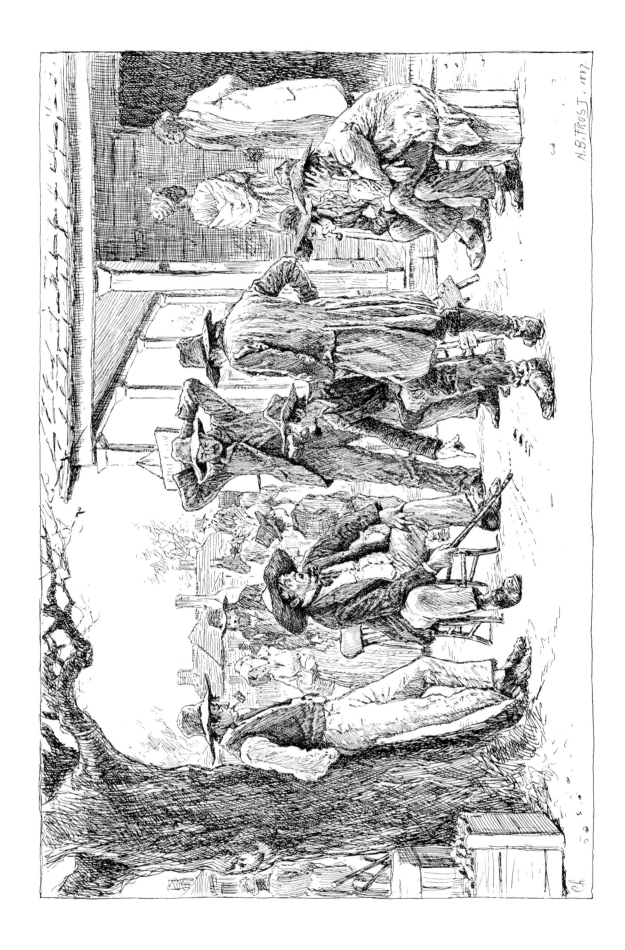

A. B. FROST. 1887.

are usually reduced to a much smaller size. The intelligent critic will of course ask what has become of the cow's other horn. My only answer is that I am sure I do not know. For a man with such a thorough knowledge of animal anatomy this omission is rather curious. His drawing of the men's hands is not as careful as Frost's or Kemble's.

Kemble's drawing contains more of his good qualities and less of his faults than almost any which I have seen. There is a very striking difference in the rendering of the old Congo woman with her brilliant shiny jet-black face—though in the drawing of it, by the way, there is not a bit of black—and the tall statuesque mulatto who stands in front of her; the action of this figure is remarkably fine. Rendering of types is Kemble's strong point, and his weak one is carelessness in detail, a carelessness which at its worst is positively aggressive The mass of wire-work to the left of the figures is thoroughly bad. It is intended for bushes or grass, but, as line-work, is meaningless. The dress of the old woman is also careless when compared with the delightful drawing in the other woman's gown. The sugar-pans and the brick oven are also careless, and the smoke is really childish. I criticise Kemble because he is such a remarkably clever draughtsman, and yet there would be no use for students to copy imperfections which with him are but the result of carelessness. With far less work he could in these details get a far better effect. Compare the tree trunk in Frost's drawing with the bushes in Kemble's and what I mean will at once be seen.

These drawings have been reproduced by Louis Chefdeville, and, like all his reproductions, are in advance of the work of any other reproductive engraver in England. He has not only reproduced the drawings excellently, but he has kept the quality of the line which each man uses. The reason of this is not difficult to find. Mr. Chefdeville is an artist and reproduces drawings in an artistic manner—that is, he seeks to reproduce the character of the draughtsman's work. His rendering of separate lines is infinitely better than that of any other English photo-engraver.

ALICE BARBER

Miss Barber's work is a good example of careful honest drawing without cleverness of handling.　She knows how to construct her figures, and she puts them
together very well.　There is a good colour scheme in her work, and the whole
drawing is simple and direct.　The only thing to criticise is a cross-hatching in
the floor which might be omitted.　The figure of the girl against the light thin
curtain is specially well drawn.　Every one knows how difficult it is to give light
clean work with a pen, and in doing this Miss Barber has been very successful.
She carries her work out more thoroughly, with a real feeling for line and without
over-elaboration, than any woman I know of.

From Harper's Magazine.—Copyright, 1881, by Harper & Brothers.

From Harper's Magazine.—Copyright, 1881, by Harper & Brothers.

From Harper's Magazine.—Copyright, 1881, by Harper & Brothers.

From Harper's Magazine.—Copyright, 1881, by Harper & Brothers.

From Harper's Magazine.—Copyright, 1881, by Harper & Brothers.

From Harper's Magazine.—Copyright, 1881, by Harper & Brothers.

ARTHUR B. FROST

CARICATURES

THESE are not models of technique—Caran D'Ache's simple outline is very much better—but the style is good enough for the purpose. They are examples of comic drawings which appeal to the whole world without any label to explain them. The only title ever tagged on to them was *Our Cat Eats Rat Poison*, which to any one with the slightest sense of humour or drawing is all-sufficient.

ROBERT BLUM

For giving a full-page photogravure to a comparatively unknown illustrator—for, I reiterate it, all illustration is unknown or ignored—and omitting to give a photogravure to Fortuny, I suppose I shall be criticised.   But I have very good reasons for doing so.   There are several drawings in existence by Fortuny which have been reproduced either by woodcuts or photo-engravings, or which as photogravures are unimportant.   I have been unable to obtain any originals. However, I should have managed to show one here, if it had not been that the Century Company loaned me the drawing of Joe Jefferson as Bob Acres by Robert Blum.   From an historical point of view, it would have been more interesting to make a photogravure from one of the Fortunys.   For the student the Blum is of much more value, for this reason.   As I have said, Fortuny lived a little too soon for the process work by which many of his followers have profited.   Among them all, there has been no more careful and at the same time more brilliant student of his work than Blum.   And this drawing was done for reproduction, while Fortuny's were not.   It therefore possesses many qualities of value to the draughtsman which are absent from the more original work of his master.   As I have also said, in almost all Fortuny's work there are smudges and blots, and though these are artistically right, they cannot be depended upon in any process-reproduction.   The Fabrès drawing, however, is a most successful exception.   Everything in this drawing of Blum's will come as nearly right as photo-engraving and printing can make it.   The photogravure is a little too hard all over.   It would be impossible to render the face more delicately than Blum has.   Notice how he gets the colour of the hair darker than the face by means of the fine lines under the modelling of it, and how he gets the tone of the face down lower than the cravat and shirt front; and how well the legs are expressed, and every line goes to show the form that is inside the breeches.   I cannot help feeling that the boots are somewhat too black, but this black is used to emphasise and bring out the delicate lights all the way from his feet to the under side of his hat.   This is a contradiction to my advice not to use too many blacks; but at the same time it is a proof of my assertion that a man who is a master of his art can do what he chooses.   The lines which surround the drawing and which in most men's hands would be a meaningless affectation of Fortuny's searching for his

forms and modelling, although they are with Blum to a certain extent an affectation,—and I doubt if he would use them to-day,—serve to bring the drawing out of the paper and to connect the black of the coat with the white of the paper without producing a hard crude line around it. Take these apparently careless lines away and you will at once discover that the drawing becomes hard and loses much in refinement. And just here I want to express another opinion. This drawing may have been made from Joe Jefferson on the stage, or studied in the studio, or done from a photograph. The fact that one cannot tell how it was done is a proof of its excellence. If a man is compelled to work from a photograph—and there are very few who can without the fact being known at once, for it is much more difficult to make a picture out of a photograph than one from nature—it is nobody's business how the work is done, nor would the use of a photograph detract from the artistic value of the drawing.

Under this head come some of Blum's drawings for Carrère and Hastings' descriptive pamphlet on the Ponce de Leon Hotel in St. Augustine, Florida, the most artistic piece of architectural drawing and hotel advertising combined I have ever seen. It is a book which should be in the hand of every architectural draughtsman. The drawings, having been made in the southern states of America, are rightly based on the work of Rico. There is not an architectural draughtsman in the world who could equal, or even come anywhere near them. Blum has given all the architectural details with the utmost fidelity, and to them he has added an artistic rendering while he has avoided all stupid results by means of his delicate play of light and shade. Interest has been added by carefully-drawn figures, and the trees and flowers are put in with a knowledge of their form in nature and not evolved from the imagination of the architectural T square brain.

ALFRED BRENNAN

BRENNAN'S work is unconventional and often startling. Much of it, of course, is but an imitation of the Fortuny manner. His skill is shown in his concentration of blacks, and in this drawing in his rendering of the Chinese weapons, about which he probably knows nothing except what he has learnt from museums; he here impresses us with the idea of a completely toned drawing, though it is not a toned drawing at all; he breaks up great spaces of light or dark by either pure black or pure white—in fact every line and touch is a triumph of technical skill combined with a thorough command of his materials and resources.

The original was a huge drawing—a drawing which took as much thought and time in execution and as much knowledge of composition as would be required to make a water-colour or oil of the same size, and there is scarcely a painter who has the technical ability to produce such a masterpiece. Because this man chooses to illustrate, his work, which the critic does not understand, is dismissed with a line. Had he made a painting of the same subject with the same amount of work in it, he would have been known all over the world. As it is, he is only an illustrator, but for pure cleverness there is no one who has ever surpassed him.

In the drawing of a stairway, which is a study in beautiful line, the lines have all the character, the meaning, and the value of the best etched line Whistler ever did. What could be better as a model for the architectural student than this?—if indeed the student could ever learn to work like Brennan. The drawing is full of interest, vitality, and distinction. There is nothing stupid and nothing photographic, and yet it was made from a photograph.

Brennan's decorative work is also filled with his individuality and character, and though, to me, much of it is absolutely incomprehensible, it is always striking and often beautiful; it is taken from any motive which he may happen to find around him, but instead of making a mere copy, he adapts this motive to his own wishes and requirements. He has illustrated several children's books and nursery rhymes, and these, when at their best, are, like his other work, technically unapproachable. Of course I know if it had not been for the influence of Fortuny, Casanova and Vierge, and the Japanese, there might not have been a

Brennan; but his power is that of filling his drawing with all sorts of opposing influences and producing a uniform whole of his own. There is probably no one living who has a greater knowledge of the requirements and limitations and possibilities of process. With the thoroughness of the Middle Age craftsman, he has studied the subject in a workshop.

From Harper's Magazine.

Copyright, 1887, by Harper & Brothers.

FREDERICK LUNGREN

LUNGREN is the third of the quartette of Americans of whom I have spoken, and though with them he was at first very much under the influence of Fortuny, Vierge, and Rico, and though his work now has many of their qualities, he has added to it, not only by his study abroad in Paris, but by uniting to the brilliancy of these Spaniards and of Frenchmen like Jean Béraud some of the methods of Germans like Schlittgen. The consequence is that while his work is in many ways suggestive of that of many men, it is at the same time his own.

What is to be specially noted in Lungren's work is the great power of expression conveyed with very few and simple lines, as well as the striking use of solid blacks, and the beauty of every line he uses. For example, in the accompanying drawing he expresses a great field with no work at all, excepting in exactly the right place, that is in the foreground, where he shows the growth of the grass and the weeds just where it would be seen, and the modelling of the ground which is given just in the right place to connect the two figures together in a good but not obtrusive manner. Notice too the use of pure blacks in the stockings and shoes of both children and in the sash and ribbons of one, and how carefully the folds of the drapery are rendered; the faces of the little girls, though perhaps not very interesting, are pretty and pleasing. The house among the trees is put in so that every line tells, while the distant wood has been drawn with chalk or crayon. The drawing itself was on smooth paper, but, as I have explained, lithographic chalk not only comes by process, but holds fairly well on this paper, which, though almost smooth, has a slight grain in the surface.

This drawing was merely an illustration for a child's story in *St. Nicholas*, and yet it is worth more study and attention—and if anything but an illustration would receive more—than a vast mass of the pictures painted every year.

HARRY FENN

It is always possible to render architecture picturesquely, even though it may be the latest American device in Queen Anne or a city shop front, if one only knows how, and Harry Fenn does. He not merely makes every line tell something, but he uses a different line for each substance. Notice how he gets the effect of the stairway with one line, the light wood of the hall with another, and how well the old chair and chest, drawn with still another, tell against it. The rug and the hangings are quite differently handled, while the fire-place in the dining-room beyond is in line and splatter work, the rest of the room in outline, which again varies the treatment. There is not such brilliant and strong colour in this drawing as in many of Fenn's, but it is an excellent example of picturesque working-out of a new, and therefore somewhat stiff interior, and, above all, of the use of line to express, not only surfaces, but the construction of a building in the best and simplest manner. Any number of Fenn's drawings can be seen in the American periodicals, especially in the *Century*. This one, however, was published in the *Magazine of Art*.

KENYON COX

KENYON COX, I believe, commenced his illustrative work with Blum, Brennan, and Lungren. But on going to France he gave up the methods which they thought to be the only right ones, that is those of intense brilliancy and cleverness, and has devoted himself to an entirely different manner of working.

Here he shows an excellent way of taking the photographic look out of a photograph, only retaining those features which give the character of the subject and suppressing all others. Thus the pose of the figure is indicated with freedom and grace, and the colour and texture of the clothes are well expressed, while the African type is self-evident. There is no obtrusive cleverness, nor indeed any cleverness of handling at all, in the drawing, but there is a very successful and serious attempt to render a type, a pose, and a costume, and the work can be thoroughly commended as good, serious, and honest, as well as for its non-photographic rendering of a photograph.

Kenyon Cox.
1885.

After photograph

WYATT EATON

Not only is this a good example of directness and freedom of line, with scarcely any cross-hatching and certainly no mechanical work, of beauty of modelling and suggestion of various surfaces, and of a man's individuality in his drawing, but it is a marvellous example of mechanical reproduction, probably the best in the book. It was engraved by the C. L. Wright Gravure Company of New York. Their aim is not, as I have found with too many other mechanical engravers, to succumb before the slightest difficulty, but, to use their own words, "to reach the acme of perfection in reproducing drawings," and, "to give an absolute fac-simile of the artist's work." It is only by such endeavours that blocks like this can be produced, that photo-engraving can advance at all.

A FEW WORDS ON PEN DRAWING

ELSEWHERE

A FEW WORDS ON PEN DRAWING
ELSEWHERE

THERE are probably good pen draughtsmen in Belgium, Holland, Austria, and Russia. But the best known artists of all these countries almost invariably leave their native land to live in Venice with Van Haanen, or in Paris with Jan Van Beers, Munkacsky, and Chelmonsky, or in London with Alma Tadema. One feels as if even a country like Austria, where the only large comparative exhibition of black and white illustrative work has ever been held,—most of its examples as shown in the Catalogue, however, were very commonplace,—is out of artistic touch with the rest of Europe. The trouble is the illustrated books and papers—the exhibition rooms of pen drawing—of these countries do not circulate all over the world, as do those of France, Germany, England, and the United States. Niccolo Masic, a Hungarian I think, and Répine, a Russian, are men whose pen work stands out in any illustrated catalogue. In Masic's there is a suggestion of Vierge. In referring to nearly all illustrated catalogues I also find that the same pictures, which have been the admiration of the *Salon*, travel around with their accompanying reproductions, from one art centre to another.

It would be impossible to write of pen drawing in Europe

and America without acknowledging the debt which all artists, who have thought and worked and striven in their art, owe to the Japanese. All know and try to reverently study the sketch-books, the drawings on silk, in fact all the decorative work of Japanese artists which is so freely and beautifully rendered by the pen, or rather by the brush. Whether these drawings are right according to instantaneous photography is of small importance; they are the most beautiful, the most decorative, the most careful studies of birds and flowers, fish and animals, ever made. I do not even pretend to know the styles, nor would it be worth while to give a catalogue of the names of Japanese artists. But I do know that one can learn more about art, decoration, and beauty from a Japanese sketch-book, which can be bought at Batsford's, High Holborn, for half-a-crown, or at John Wanamaker's, Philadelphia, for fifty cents, than is often to be learned from a whole season of modern European picture-galleries. In making this assertion I am sure I should have the support of men like Habert-Dys, Felix Régamey, Alfred Brennan, Frederick Lungren, Abbey, and Parsons, as well as that of the commissioners, appointed by the Japanese Government, who have just said, in their report, that there is very little to learn in European art to-day.

But unless one can assimilate Japanese methods to one's own requirements, in the manner of Brennan and Habert-Dys,—that is, unless one can engraft Japanese methods on European subjects, —it is better simply to study their drawings as an old master's pen work might be studied. Otherwise the result would be a medley, neither Japanese nor European, with about the value of a tea-chest made in Birmingham.

I have no intention, however, of attempting a detailed account or analysis of Japanese pen drawing, for so different is it from European work that it would require a volume apart, and several very able books on Japanese art are to be had.

After examining carefully the wonderful collection of Japanese drawings shown in the Burlington Fine Arts Club in the spring of 1888, I cannot help thinking that it might be better for western artists to give up drawing with a pen and take to the brush—that is, I mean, the brush used by the Chinese and Japanese. We should get better effects of certain kinds with a brush than we can with a pen. In their making and reproduction of pen drawings, the Japanese are hundreds of years ahead of us in other ways. Their ink is better than any we have, their wood-engravers are far more sympathetic, reverent, and careful than even the fac-simile men of America, and their printing is excellent.[1]

[1] I see no reason to alter what I have said after seeing the Paris Exhibition. The display of printed books, drawings, and engravings was very large and complete. But it did not show me that any other but the countries I have mentioned possesses a great and original illustrator.

ARCHITECTURAL PEN DRAWING

ARCHITECTURAL PEN DRAWING

ARCHITECTURAL drawing to-day is not artistic. Of course architects would explain that it is not intended to be so; but I maintain that in one of its branches it should be, and it is of this only that I have any right to speak. I am not an architect, and therefore I am not qualified to criticise technical architectural drawing.

But, on referring to Mr. R. Phené Spiers's book on the subject, which has just appeared, I find he says that the term architectural drawing "is intended to include every kind of drawing which may have to be executed by an architect at any period of his career, whether for the purposes of elementary study, professional practice, or recreation." As such a variety covers all sorts of artistic and mechanical work, I feel myself as free to speak of the artistic side as Mr. Spiers himself.

Architectural draughtsmen have opportunities of making artistic drawings, but they seldom take advantage of them. Nor is this, as is sometimes supposed, because exactness prevents their seeing the picturesque, or rather the artistic side of architectural drawing. The truth is they are often much less exact than artists, for the simple reason that they know too much. They understand so well how a building should be, that they do not see it as it is. As a very striking example of what I say, I would refer the reader to the

American Architect for 23d July 1887, in which the results of
a competition were published. A photograph of an old house in
Normandy had been given as a subject, and of the dozen or more
drawings made from it by as many draughtsmen, none had the
slightest pretensions to architectural exactness or artistic truth, or
more especially to technical knowledge of pen drawing, save those
drawn by Harry Fenn and J. D. Woodward, the only artists
represented. I have before me at this moment a drawing by a
Royal Academician of a recently erected public building, in which
he has been careful to omit certain prominent and very artistic
details of his own, in order to insert the stone jointing which,
if actually true, would make each stone as big as an Egyptian
monolith.

The drawings to which I refer were not working drawings
intended for architects only, but were meant to be shown to the
general public. If it be said they were done to the best of the
ability of the architectural draughtsmen this is but a proof of my
assertion that architects to-day are not artistic draughtsmen. Of
course I am not here concerned with working drawings, details,
and perspectives for the architect's own use, which are technical
architectural drawings and not drawings of architecture—a difference
pointed out by the late Mr. E. W. Godwin. But there is no reason
why the drawings architects make for the public or for their clients
should not be artistic. Mr. Spiers says the public, as a rule, fail
" to estimate correctly from a drawing of any description the proportion, mass, or scale of a building." He then says, farther on,
that in competition for an exhibition, however, the object is " to set
off the drawing in an *attractive manner.*" (The italics are his.)
" The finish of the drawing and the method by which this is attained,
whether in pen and ink or tinting in monochrome or colours, is
consequently of some importance." He again says, " A study of
an important building, in which colour forms the chief element of
its beauty, as in one of the Venetian palaces, St. Mark's at Venice,
Giotto's tower at Florence, or a portion of the interior of the church
at Assisi, may claim long expenditure of time, because these subjects
are worth it, and art as well as nature (or the effect produced by age)
have contributed to their beauty." On the whole, Mr. Spiers's book
only shows that he does appreciate the fact, though he is loath, as is

almost every architect, to acknowledge it, that architectural drawing must be artistic if it is to have any value. He also quotes Mr. Ware, who says that architectural drawing lies between mechanical and artistic draughtsmanship; therefore unless a student has studied both mechanical and artistic draughtsmanship, as he does in the Massachusetts Institute of Technology,—Mr. Ware's school,—I should very much like to know how he is to tell when he is either mechanical or artistic. That the architectural student commonly knows nothing about artistic drawing—in London at any rate—Mr. Spiers himself admits, since he says that probably not more than one per cent of the articled pupils here avail themselves of the opportunity of attending the schools of art.

In looking into the three divisions of architectural drawing as defined by an architect, Mr. Maurice B. Adams,[1] it is clear that but one—that which includes working plans and details—is exclusively technical. These are not for exhibition or publication any more than are the anatomical studies of the painter. Detail drawings and elevations are the anatomical drawings of architecture. But it is quite different with drawings prepared for clients or exhibition, in which what is needed is picturesque and graphic perspective, as well as exactness. That even to architects they do not answer the purpose of working drawings is easily to be seen, since the draughtsman, to make them intelligible architecturally, has to supplement them with a frieze of plans and elevations. And certainly clients and public would take more interest and pleasure in them if the perspective drawings were picturesque as well as conventionally correct. But if the architectural draughtsman is to attain this picturesqueness, if he is to be concerned with his sky-lines and "the general massing of parts for effect," he must have knowledge of something beyond the mere construction of elevations. He must do as he is made to do in the Massachusetts Institute of Technology, for example: study decoration, perspective, the point of view, outline, interiors, etc.; quite as important, if an artistic result is to be attained, as a knowledge of the resisting power of wood or metal which any engineer understands ten times as much about as any architect. He must be not simply an

---

[1] Lecture on Architectural Drawing delivered before the Royal Institute of British Architects, and published in the Transactions of that Society.

architect but an artist as well, and if artists cannot be made, neither can architects. Mr. Adams seems to realise the increasing tendency to forget this fact. He says, " It seems to me more than ever desirable in this essentially commercial age of push and steam, to take particular care lest we allow the science of building to crush out the higher and nobler spirit which constitutes the life and character of our Art." Mr. Walter Millard in a paper read before the Architectural Association was even more emphatic on the subject. " Every day," he declared, " it seems to be more generally understood, that the first thing necessary for good architecture is that the architects must be artists. Good designs are not to be produced by accident any more than good pictures or good sculpture, but by men endowed with artistic ability, who have taken all care to cultivate it to the utmost."

But it is not merely for the benefit of clients and public that architects should aim to become artistic draughtsmen. If they are unable to draw—that is, see artistically—they cannot build artistically, and here again I may quote Mr. Adams. " If," he says, " drawing for the architect is only at best a means to an end, we must, if we aim at good architecture, have correspondingly able and sympathetic draughtsmanship." Mr. Burges also urged the artistic training of architects. He even went so far as to say[1] " no amount of architectural drawing would make a man an artist or an architect, unless he knows the human figure. When the Institute draws for itself instead of going to past ages, we may have an architecture." Mr. Millard advocates the " habit of sketching" in the student or draughtsman of architecture, because it " must tend to bring out whatever artistic ability he may happen to be endowed with, to accustom his eye to appreciate delicacies of form, subtlety of proportion, and beauty of composition, and all those niceties that go to make just the difference between the work of an artist and a 'cobbler'; thereby to set him thinking and rouse his imagination; and in a word, to at once furnish him with ideas, and give him skill and readiness in expressing them."

Of the architects of to-day Mr. Ernest George, who has a world-wide reputation among architects as a draughtsman, builds houses which have the most character of their own. This was

---

[1] Paper on Architectural Drawing, published in Transactions of the R. I. B. A. for 1860-61.

also the case with Mr. Richardson in America. That details can be drawn artistically, as well as accurately, thus interesting not only architects but artists also, is shown by the careful, beautiful drawing of a capital by Mr. Spiers, published in the Transactions of the Royal Institute of British Artists, and by the wonderful detail drawing of the porch of St. Paul's by Mr. Schultz. And though these are merely technical drawings for the benefit of architects, they are filled with the feeling for art, and real love for the artistic possibilities, and beauty of the subject drawn. But to call the slovenly notes by Mr. Street,[1] which may have been useful to himself, an admirable example of a useful drawing, or the checker-board windows of Mr. Norman Shaw's perspectives fine, makes one admire the half-trained, but very ambitious, efforts of a man like Mr. Beresford Pite, to cut himself loose from such very careless masters.

For the last hundred years or more, English and American architects have been trained apart, without coming within artistic influence, with the result shown in the buildings which line the streets of American and English cities. The trouble is that architects must be business men first, social swells next, and then engineers, sanitary authorities, builders and surveyors,—if they happen to have a slight knowledge of art, it will not do them any harm. Architecture in our times is too much of a business, too little of an art. Like the law, it has become a good opening for impecunious younger sons. As Mr. Millard says, if architecture is "nothing less than the entire profession of building-surveying, with a knowledge of the quality and market value of all kinds of material and labour sufficient for an enterprising contractor; a grasp of physical science, constructive formulæ, and methods

---

[1] Mr. Street is responsible for the greater part of the present slovenliness of architectural drawing in England. He not only drew very carelessly, though probably well enough to suit his own ends, but he was one of those men who insist that an architect must do everything for himself, even down to the most trifling and mechanical details. Instead of getting artists to draw his perspectives, he always drew them himself. They may, even if not artistic, have answered his purpose, but unfortunately they have given him the reputation of being master of a subject—drawing and sketching—of which he was not even a proficient pupil. The worst of it is, that drawings which he probably would be ashamed to show, were he alive, are published in architectural journals as models for students, with the result that in the last few years, architectural drawing has greatly degenerated.

of calculation so essential to an engineer; acquaintance with
authorities, and skill in expounding the mysteries of easements
and arbitrations, compensations and contracts, and cases of 'ancient
lights,' such that a lawyer might envy; as well as a general capacity
for conducting affairs of all management of property, insurance
agency, or advertising; in fact so many and such varied accomplishments,—the wonder is, what room there can be left for architecture
proper."

In looking over years of architectural work, I do not see any
drawings which, artistically, can equal those made by professional
illustrators who have absolutely no pretensions to architectural
science. The consequence is, I can only recommend to the student
of architectural pen drawing the work of these illustrators. Some
architects, especially in America, — M'Kim, Meade and White,
Carrère and Hastings, for example,—have their perspectives drawn
by artists, and an art which in the hands of its own craftsmen
is perfectly stupid, by artistic draughtsmen has been made attractive
to the public, as well as to architects themselves. Notable
examples of this are the illustrations for Mrs. Van Renssalaer's
series on American Architecture in the *Century*, and M. Camille
Piton's drawings in *Harper's;* and all or nearly all these drawings
were made by painters or draughtsmen; while there are many
French illustrators, such as Lucien Gautier and H. Scott, whose
work is equally good. If this were done more frequently, and
such drawings were hung at the Royal Academy, there would
be less complaint that the public does not appreciate architectural
drawing. The public does not care for technical drawings, which,
though good from an architectural standpoint, are utterly unintelligible to all but architects, any more than it would prefer
an anatomical study to a portrait. One cannot be expected to
admire in a drawing trees which look like masses of wire work
or wooden toy trees; or the graceful lines of a beautiful building,
when drawn as if from a balloon or the bottom of a well. Neither
can one enjoy drawings set up with all the crudities and imperfections of the draughtsmanship of three or four hundred years
ago; or drawings perfectly artless in execution, in which all the
laws of light and shade are ignored, even though the buildings
represented may look brand-new, and have all the jointing of their

Carrère & Hastings, Architects
New York

THE ALCAZAR—ST. AUGUSTINE, FLORIDA

stone-work carefully drawn out. In the Architectural Gallery of the Royal Academy of 1887 I only remember two or three drawings which appealed to me: one water-colour by Mr. Lessore, and pencil and wash drawings by Mr. Arnold B. Mitchell. The pen drawings were utterly uninteresting and inartistic, and yet when you came to look at them, you saw that artistic results could have been had in all, without in the least detracting from their architectural value. I must again repeat that I speak in this chapter only of drawings published and exhibited to the public, or made for clients, and which need not necessarily be subject to conventional architectural laws.

Architects should give up showing the public inartistic representations of what may have been artistic originals, and instead, have their buildings photographed, confining themselves to their often very beautiful working drawings for practical purposes; or better still, secure the aid of an artistically trained draughtsman; or, best of all, arrange their system of architectural education so that the coming generation of architects will know some little about art, and not become mere business men with no artistic appreciation of the profession of architecture. But, as I have said, I cannot mention a single architectural draughtsman of to-day whose work I would recommend to students who wish to make artistic pen drawings of architecture. In this connection architects will probably note the omission of several well-known names. I probably know the work of these men as well as architects themselves. But artistically it does not compare with that of the illustrators upon whose style theirs is modelled.

Even at meetings of architects, drawings by artists are shown as models of what the drawing of architecture should be. I cannot but differ, however, from architects who uphold Turner as a model, simply because Mr. Ruskin has said that he "leads to rightness." This cannot be believed by any one who has studied Turner's work, and the buildings which he drew or painted. I can think of no worse architectural work for artists or architects to study than that of Turner. He cared to show places and buildings, not as they really are, but as it pleased him that they should look. Rightness was nothing to him. He was never half so accurate as Mr. Ruskin himself.

Finally, in its greatest days, architecture was an art practised by painters and sculptors; so it must be to be an art at all. To think that any one can make an architectural drawing, to say nothing of building a house of any artistic value, without being an artist, is absurd. One cannot produce art work until after years of patient study, and in order to secure artistic results, one has got to know what good drawing is, and then be able to do it.

Probably architects will suppose that I intend setting up as a rival to Lord Grimthorpe. But the reason I write as I do is because I have such a great respect for artistic architecture. When one sees around one all traces of old London, or rather of old England, disappearing under the puny hands of knighted and titled jerry builders, drain constructors and sanitary engineers; when the old churches of the city rise up from their beauty, scraped, white-washed, and re-arranged according to the ideas of these decorators, house-painters, and upholsterers, one can do nothing but utter what of course will be an unavailing protest against the unchecked sway of the building trade, into which architecture in this country is degenerating.

PEN DRAWING FOR BOOK

DECORATION

PEN DRAWING FOR BOOK DECORATION

RECENTLY certain artists have sought to separate the conventional decoration of books from their pictorial illustration, and to treat each as a distinct art. Though, in a measure, the illustrator has become divorced from the decorator, there is no real reason for this separation. In the greatest age of book decoration, I believe the decorator and illustrator worked together, and were in the best examples one and the same man. No one would ever deny that Dürer or Holbein, Mantegna or Bellini, or whoever illustrated many of the beautiful books from the Aldine press, was not both decorator and illustrator; if the work was not actually done by the same hand, it was the product of the same mind. No one but a master of anatomy, of figure drawing, could have produced the figures which are interwoven in the decoration of almost all these works. I refer, not to the pictures inserted in the text, in the initial letters or in the margins, but to the conventional decorative figures themselves. Neither do

I mean to say that Dürer did all the work with his own hand; I would as soon assert that he drew and cut all his wood blocks, but he invented it, sketched it and touched it up. And as with Dürer, so with the other great book decorators in the past.

But while I have no intention of separating the illustrator and the decorator, since I believe no such separation should be recognised, there is a distinction between drawings which, while they ornament the text, are specially intended for its elucidation, and those which, though they may illustrate the text, are intended primarily to ornament the page according to conventional rules. Of these latter I propose to speak here. Of the drawings reproduced in other chapters, there is not one which would not be a decoration in any book; many I now give are illustrative; and yet a certain difference in motives and in treatment, even when conventional laws are set aside, is apparent.

The old MSS., the missals, and early printed books were treated very much as are modern illustrated publications. The MSS. were made rich with ornament, sometimes confined to a very elaborate initial letter, sometimes extending down the margins, and they also contained many pictures wholly realistic in treatment, either placed in the page very much as are the cuts in our magazines, or else so interwoven with the ornament as to be almost inseparable from it. And so it was with the early printed books. At times the text was enclosed in a border of graceful spirals or purely conventional forms; at others it enclosed

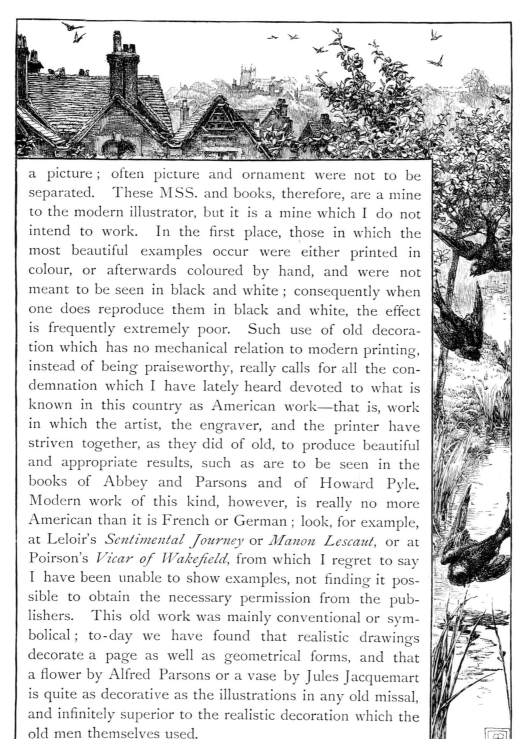

a picture; often picture and ornament were not to be separated. These MSS. and books, therefore, are a mine to the modern illustrator, but it is a mine which I do not intend to work. In the first place, those in which the most beautiful examples occur were either printed in colour, or afterwards coloured by hand, and were not meant to be seen in black and white; consequently when one does reproduce them in black and white, the effect is frequently extremely poor. Such use of old decoration which has no mechanical relation to modern printing, instead of being praiseworthy, really calls for all the condemnation which I have lately heard devoted to what is known in this country as American work—that is, work in which the artist, the engraver, and the printer have striven together, as they did of old, to produce beautiful and appropriate results, such as are to be seen in the books of Abbey and Parsons and of Howard Pyle. Modern work of this kind, however, is really no more American than it is French or German; look, for example, at Leloir's *Sentimental Journey* or *Manon Lescaut*, or at Poirson's *Vicar of Wakefield*, from which I regret to say I have been unable to show examples, not finding it possible to obtain the necessary permission from the publishers. This old work was mainly conventional or symbolical; to-day we have found that realistic drawings decorate a page as well as geometrical forms, and that a flower by Alfred Parsons or a vase by Jules Jacquemart is quite as decorative as the illustrations in any old missal, and infinitely superior to the realistic decoration which the old men themselves used.

a Description of

Morning in LONDON.

A second reason for not giving examples of old book decoration is that, even when not coloured, it was drawn on the wood and seldom engraved by the artist himself, and therefore, to a certain extent, was not autographic. Of course drawing on the wood in the time of Dürer and Holbein, especially when intended for the decoration of the text, was more or less conventional, as a reference to the etched work of the same men will show. The artist, when working for the engraver, could, by drawing less freely, do much to help him to obtain accurate results and to lighten his labour. As we are often reminded, artists and crafts-men then worked together. Books were produced entirely by art workmen in a workshop, a beautiful example of which remains to-day in the Plantin Museum at Antwerp, with its type-founding rooms, its artists' designing rooms and designs, its printing presses, and its "hutches" for tame authors and artists and proof-readers; it was the house, the home, and the workshop of the publisher. But save that publishers and authors and artists do not live on the premises, the same

state of affairs, carried out in a much broader manner than even Plantin would have thought possible, will be found in many of the great publishing houses to-day. However, because we see the business details and the shoppy working of such firms, and because they have produced results undreamed of by Dürer or Plantin, only the beautiful side of whose work survives, we younger men are told by unsuccessful engravers, visionary dreamers, incompetent middlemen, or mediocre illustrators, that we must go back to the time of Dürer, that we must give up our improved printing presses, our process work, our overlays, and our art for the people, made by the people and enjoyed by the people, and return to the work which was made only for the few and given to the few—to the fine illustrated volumes intended rather as curiosities for presentation to popes and kings and nobles, than books which the people, or even artists, should ever see. If this is to be, why should we stop with the Renaissance, with the decorative work of Rome, with those mummy cases of Egypt which show how much more the Greeks knew about painting than Giotto, or why should we look at the beauty of Greek art at all? Why, the reasoning of these people would carry us back to painting ourselves blue and drawing with a burnt stick on the walls of a cave.

The great difference between the conditions of early and modern book-making is too often lost sight of, and yet, without understanding it, it is impossible to justly value the great development accomplished in

illustration and decoration within the last few years. The old illustrators attempted the same scheme of illustration as that which is carried out to-day; they would have used the same realism had it been possible —or the same idealism, whichever you choose to call it, for I suppose it is universally admitted that between idealism and realism of the highest kind there is no difference;—they arranged their pages in the same manner, a manner which is praised in their work and condemned in ours; but they had not the same technical knowledge or the same mechanical facilities. To begin with, the methods of the printers of the fifteenth century could not be applied to the large editions of to-day. The old books, which either were carefully chained in one place or were the rare possessions of the great of the earth, could be decorated to any extent; their size was not an important consideration. But if the books of to-day—intended for wide circulation—were equally decorated, with every page of text enclosed in a border as in books of the fifteenth and sixteenth centuries, they would be so swollen as to be almost entirely unmanageable. This is a fact regretted by a select few, though even if the old methods could be applied to modern editions, they would not equal those now adopted. We are told much about Caxton and Dürer, Holbein and Plantin. But were these men living to-day, instead of looking back to Gutenberg and MS. illuminators who were their pre-decessors, they would use steam presses and avail themselves of every appliance of mechanics, science and art, as they did in their own day, thus

placing themselves far in advance of their time and their contemporaries. The draughtsman to-day who is most in sympathy with Dürer is he who adapts his work to the methods of Theodore de Vinne in New York or the Guillaume Frères in Paris. It is owing to the progressive men who have not spent their time lamenting the past and mourning present degeneracy, but have always sought to advance, that the world has developed at all. To have the inventions and improvements of to-day called bad because they were mechanical impossibilities three hundred years ago is rubbish ; and it is on such rubbish that modern art is nourished.

For a time, especially about the beginning of this century, it seemed as if the art of book decoration was dormant. There was, it is true, what was accepted as decoration, but it was really desecration. Old books were borrowed from unreservedly and their designs used without the least sense of fitness or proportion. A publisher would not have hesitated to embellish a cook-book with head and tail pieces from the Divine Comedy. He employed decorators — really desecrators — to scrawl all over the inside and outside of his book covers, and to spread themselves unrestrainedly on the pages in the most obnoxious manner. This sort of thing came to a crisis in the Books of Beauty. The consequence was that many draughtsmen in disgust gave up all attempt at decoration. But within the last few years a new impetus has been given to the decoration of books,—using the term to express the dis-

LET NOT THE FLOWERS OF SPRING PASS VS BY LET VS CROWN OVR SELVES WITH ROSES BEFORE THEY BE WITHERED

tinction I have pointed out,—and it is to this modern work that I will pay most attention, since it alone, having been done for reproduction by process, comes within my present scope.

The principal conventional motives were very early evolved in every country; we have, as a rule, endeavoured to make little or no advance upon them, and they are still accepted as standards only admissible of slight changes. This, however, is far from meaning that all that is possible to-day is to copy what has already been done. No matter how conventional the treatment or what the motive, the decoration should have some relation not only to the size and shape of the page, but to the subject of the text. If we surround our pages with designs of the sixteenth century—as some draughtsmen still do and would have all others do—which have no relation to the text, it is not decoration but senseless display. Dürer's designs for the *Missal of Maximilian* might be appropriate to a nineteenth-century prayer-book, but there must be a great lack of ideas on the part of the nineteenth-century illustrator who cannot work into sixteenth-century forms nineteenth-century feeling. It is always wise to go to Dürer, to Meckenen, to Mantegna, or to any of the illustrators of the fifteenth and sixteenth centuries for motives, but to literally copy their designs and to print them on a modern page reveals an absolute sterility of invention or a conservative servility which is disgusting. The accompanying cuts of the two little angels carrying the crown and St. George and the Dragon show how admirably some of Dürer's work would be adapted to many of our needs; but on looking through Howard Pyle's *Otto of the Silver Hand*, one finds the little tail-pieces there have much the same motives and are carried out in much the same spirit, and yet are altogether original in subject, while they are reproduced mechanically with an ease which would have surprised Dürer. There is probably no draughtsman as successful as Howard Pyle in working in the manner of the sixteenth-century artists, always, however, adding something distinctly his own. His mediæval tales have given him good reason to adhere to the old models. The book I have just mentioned

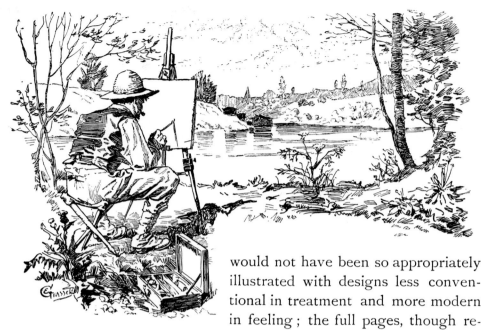

would not have been so appropriately illustrated with designs less conventional in treatment and more modern in feeling ; the full pages, though reproduced by process, look like old wood blocks ; the head and tail pieces at a glance might be mistaken for Dürer's. But that Pyle knows how utterly out of place these designs would be in books relating to other periods is proved by the very different methods he employs for other subjects. His *Pepper and Salt* gives an excellent idea of the great extent of his knowledge and his perfect understanding of the limitations and possibilities of the decoration of a page.

An equally good example of the perfect use of old methods engrafted on modern work is to be found in the cover—too large to be reproduced here—of any number of the *Münchener Kalender*. In it again all the old feeling is preserved, and yet we find the proper adaptation to modern requirements in the coat of arms, the eagle, and the emblems of the printer by whom it is issued. But still, I cannot help saying that from my standpoint at any rate, such schemes of decoration as those by Grasset are even more appropriate. In his work we have, in the first place, the old decorative line in the borders, in the centre are the charming little suggestions of a picture carried out exactly in the way the old men would have done it, realistic figures and landscape being given in a shape which accords with, and decorates and illustrates the page at the same time. A realistic picture can be just as decorative as any number of conventional lines. The illustrations of the earlier illustrators seem more conventional to us, simply because technical conditions allowed them less freedom than is now possible. I say and I maintain that there is no earthly reason, save narrow, conservative, hide-bound tradition or inability to draw,

which prevents the modern man from producing decoration of this sort. The designs are not only well drawn, but are perfectly appropriate in their places, and they prove Grasset's power to produce decoration which has some relation to the nineteenth century as well as to the Catalogue of the Paris *Salon* which he was illustrating; just as the decorative illustrations of sixteenth-century artists had some relation to their time. The mixing up of conventionalism and realism in decoration is to be found in almost any old book.

But because, if I may so express it, realism prevails in the decorative work of Alfred Parsons, though he is able to draw flowers as no one else ever drew them, and to fill his page with the mingling of decoration and realism that Dürer never dreamt of, though his every line is as beautiful as Dürer's, are we not to use it, not to study it? As far as I can see, the only reason why it should be considered not altogether right is because it is produced to-day, and because there is no one else in the world who can do anything like it. It is interesting to compare the photogravure after Parsons in the English Chapter with the designs by Walter Crane worked out in such a different spirit. The organic lines in the latter are very beautiful, but the Parsons' plate, and also the heading *In Shakespeare's*

"we have no souls and   we are gay without care"

Country, show there is
of decorative drawing
think a great deal better
to books published to-
Crane's work are two
made, not for any
Messrs. Clark, that is
Fine as all are, they
tion of two, absolutely
can see, to the work of
er or the publisher, and
itself to any one.   On
Echoes of Hellas, he
his splendid ideas of
design is appropriate.
out that he seems to
dern life and feeling to
referring only to his
notable examples in
in doing this are the

another and newer way
which I, for my part,
and more appropriate
day.   The examples of
of a series of designs
special books, but for
for   trade   purposes.
have, with the excep-
no relation, as far as I
the printer, the engrav-
a design should explain
the other hand, in his
has really carried out
decoration, while the
I simply want to point
object to applying mo-
decoration.   I am here
pen drawing.   The only
which he has succeeded
old cover of *St. Nicholas*

and the cover of the *Chants of Labour*.   But even in them there is a con-
ventionality for which I do not admit the necessity.   I do not consider
that conventional or geometrical lines are more decorative than any
others ; and this, Parsons' work proves, as also does that of men like
Caran D'Ache and Rochegrosse and Mars, who work the life of to-day
into their initials and decorations instead of trying to copy old conven-
tionality.   Look at the swallow by Habert-Dys, or the tail-pieces by Unger.

Shakspeare's Country.

The Old Falcon Inn at Bidford.

EACH number of the *English Illustrated Magazine* has always contained reproductions of old work and new designs which were appropriate to, and specially designed for, the articles they decorated. Among them I cannot help mentioning— though they are not drawn in pen and ink—several by A. C. Morrow for articles on different industries ; these were most decorative and most appropriate, and I only regret they were not done in pen and ink, so that I might use them. Caldecott and Herbert Railton and Hugh Thomson, the two latter in their *Coaching Ways and Coaching Days*, have produced head and tail pieces which were most appropriate, as well as good in design. But the best decorative work in the *English Illustrated* is to be seen in many drawings by Alfred Parsons, Heywood Sumner, and Henry Ryland. To my mind Heywood Sumner's illustrations to his article on Undine are the most beautiful decorations it has yet published. And if all of his drawings are worked out in a more quaint than decora- tive style, they often convey the ideas of the life, character, and feeling of the time and country he was illustrating or decorating, though some- times, notably in *The Besom-Maker*, he seems to have striven only to perpetuate the imperfections and crudities.

A set of men in England who have persistently set themselves up solely as conventional decorators are the artists of the Century Guild, and three of their designs they have kindly loaned me. Selwyn Image, Arthur Mackmurdo, and Herbert Horne are the best known of these men who, to me in an incomprehensible manner, refuse to make use of any of the adjuncts with which science has in our time furnished the book-maker. The full page drawing of Diana is so remarkably well done that one sees, if it were not that Herbert Horne refuses to make

SILVARVM·POTENS·D

IANA·CANDIDA·DEA·

himself comprehensible to the ordinary mortal, he might easily do much more good in the world and fill a far wider sphere than the narrow niche in which he deliberately places himself. It would be difficult to explain in what way

 art is served by using bad paper; and from the standpoint of printing illustrations, the paper of the *Hobby-Horse* is thoroughly bad, handmade papers of all sorts being unsuitable for the printing of pen drawings, or any illustrations printed from blocks, in fact. The initial by Horne is of equal value with that by Bridwell given farther on, but it is no better. The tailpiece also is extremely good, that is, the spaces are well kept. It may have some hidden meaning; to me, however, its only meaning is the beauty of line. Nor do I understand the printing of the *Hobby-Horse* page; it is very good as a mass, but very bad for practical purposes, that is, for reading. In many of the decorative designs, notably the cover by Selwyn Image, I fail to grasp the significance or to discover any relation to any age; and certainly, if Dürer was right, the *Hobby-Horse* men are all wrong. I prefer to believe that a man like Albert Dürer, whose work was understood by the people of his age, or Parsons, whose work is understood by those of to-day, really does more good than one whose designs can only be made intelligible by a continual reference to the history of symbolism.

Those who have strong faith in the degeneracy of modern art often contend that we cannot make purely decorative initials equal to those of the men of the sixteenth century. That the initials of the old men were very beautiful and very decorative no one would be foolish enough to deny.

 OREOVER, that in the original drawings there was far more refinement than could be given in the woodcuts, we know from the little blocks with the drawings on them, for one reason or another left uncut, and now to be seen in the Plantin Museum. In delicacy of execution this work is very much akin to modern pen drawing, and would be reviled, was its existence known to them, by those who now can find praise only for the really excessively bad reproductions of that early period. Indeed, there is no better proof of the fact that, before the days of process, much of the draughtsman's work was lost in the cutting than a comparison between these drawings on the block and the

printed initials of the same date, while the realistic treatment in the original drawing also shows that much of the old conventionalism was due to the limitations of the woodcutter. But that the designing of initials is not a lost art is demonstrated by reference to the initials by Bridwell, designed for and published in the *Century Magazine*, two of which the Century Company have allowed me to reproduce, as well as those by the Century Guild artists to which I have just referred. They are quite equal to any initials ever designed. The actual drawing in Bridwell's lines might in places be somewhat firmer, but it must be admitted that some of Dürer's work of this kind is about as slovenly as possible. Take Bridwell's letter S, for an initial to decorate an article on nature, or more especially on a pine wood, could anything

be more appropriate? And it is utterly and entirely different in motive from the other; one is classic, while the other shows the free motive of the Japanese.

I have not published any Japanese designs because they are not appropriate to a European work, not having been designed for it. But it is quite as admissible to use Japanese as classical motives, if we can adapt them to our purpose. Neither have I given any of the Europeanised Japanese of Felix Régamey who, of course, did so much to introduce this style to western illustrators. His work to me is always purely that of a European who attempts to be Japanese, and not the engrafting of European ideas on Japanese motives.

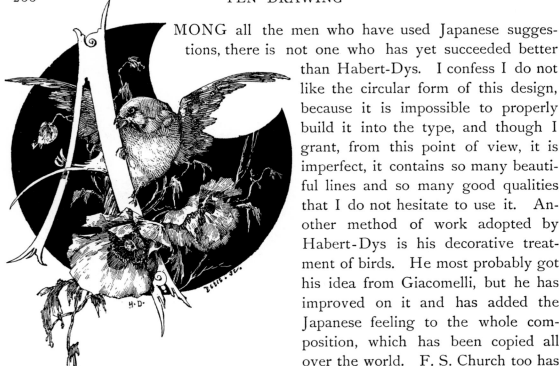

MONG all the men who have used Japanese suggestions, there is not one who has yet succeeded better than Habert-Dys. I confess I do not like the circular form of this design, because it is impossible to properly build it into the type, and though I grant, from this point of view, it is imperfect, it contains so many beautiful lines and so many good qualities that I do not hesitate to use it. Another method of work adopted by Habert-Dys is his decorative treatment of birds. He most probably got his idea from Giacomelli, but he has improved on it and has added the Japanese feeling to the whole composition, which has been copied all over the world. F. S. Church too has worked out this idea, but I do not think really as well as Habert-Dys. The little drawings of a cock fight by Renouard are as Japanese as they can be, but yet no Jap would have drawn them exactly like this. They are as French as they are Japanese.

IRECT copying is, I insist, always bad, but in the initial and the tail-piece by Bracquemond there is most skilful combination of German and Japanese, while the whole result is French.

Not only the time but a country's national characteristics can be perfectly easily expressed in book decoration. The two designs by E. Unger are as German as they possibly can be. A good deal of the tree drawing is bad and careless, though much of this may be due to the woodcutting, for it was drawn on wood. But the spaces are well filled, there is absolutely no mistaking the Munich model who has posed for the figure. The same can be said of the drawing by Walter Crane for the *Chants of Labour*, to which I have already called attention, where the workman is most characteristically an Englishman, and where the whole space is better filled than in the example of Unger's work, and the design is a great deal more appropriate, for Unger's was made to be used as a head-piece in

Universum very much in the same manner as Walter Crane's designs were drawn for Messrs. Clark.

I have said nothing as yet about decorative lettering. The pages of MSS.

and early printed books are often held up as models, but effective as they are from a decorative stand-point, they are only too frequently extremely difficult to read, and, whatever books may have been to their owners in the fifteenth and sixteenth centuries, they to-day are intended above all to be read. Those who believe decoration must be primarily useful, cannot but admit that a legible page is of far more value than a beautiful page which is unreadable. The MSS. are often, simply in their lettering, far more beautiful than any printed books. But the men who are held up to-day as masters of book decoration were only too ready to sacrifice this beauty in order to make use of the invention of printing, and by it to save time and labour. The profession of the scribe was doomed from the moment the first printed book was published. Just as the illustrators after Gutenberg recognised the folly of having the

text, which accompanied their drawings, cut on wood instead of being set up in type, so it would be useless for the illustrator of the modern magazine to

seek to return to the methods of the first printers. There is not much doubt that a book with all the lettering reproduced from the MSS. would be much more trying for readers than a book with all the text set up in type. However, for an occasional page or for a title page, the artists' lettering instead of the ordinary type is very charming. Walter Crane works, probably to a greater extent than any one else, in this manner. But I do not altogether like his lettering; it is nearly always the same, it is not easy to read, and I do not think it is well spaced. Compare the sameness of his or Heywood Sumner's lettering with the infinite variety used by Alfred Parsons, or Howard Pyle, or Alfred Brennan. The latter vary their lettering to suit their text, and this Walter Crane and Heywood Sumner never do. Nor do they even draw it carefully. Though they believe type and decoration to be of equal importance they slight the lettering.

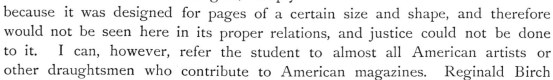

Many examples of good conventional decorative work I cannot give, simply because it was designed for pages of a certain size and shape, and therefore would not be seen here in its proper relations, and justice could not be done to it. I can, however, refer the student to almost all American artists or other draughtsmen who contribute to American magazines. Reginald Birch

has done much work which is filled with the feeling of the German Renaissance, in him developed by study in Munich. Ludwig S. Ipsen has brought his knowledge of Celtic art to the decoration of American books, where, however, one feels it to be a foreign element. Roger Riordan's designs for stained glass ought to be mentioned in this connection, for, reproduced in black and white, they become beautiful page decorations. George Wharton Edwards' decorative pen work is frequently very good, though it is not always very original. It would be an unpardonable omission to leave out Elihu Vedder, the greatest American decorator, in some ways the greatest decorator of modern times, if I were concerned with all forms of book decoration. But I am only treating of pen work, and Vedder seldom

LII.

SINCE. when Time's brooding bird did patient sit
Upon her sphered egg, the world, to wit,
    Potent with life, in ocean, earth, & air,
    Ere ever faun or flower did people it:

LIIj.

Since when from countless germs life's tree did grow
    From writhing worms about its roots below,
    From dragon-shapes that clasp its fossil stem,
    To bear love's fruit, & human flowers arow.

LIV.

                                                    [dwell,
Where Thought's winged kind among its branches
    Still fertilized by Beauty's potent spell;
    Cast & re-cast in Nature's supple mould,
    Through death & change, & birth's transforming cell.

LV.

                                                    [space,
'Twas pictured here — with boughs outspread thro'
Blossomed with stars upon the sky's swart face,
    With globing worlds for fruit, that cool or glow
    As night & day, like leaves their shadows chase.

works with a pen, nor is his brush work carried out with the pen feeling. In France the late Paul Baudry did some very fine book decoration, but, as far as I know, his life was not devoted to this work, of which he has left comparatively few examples. Much the same can be said of Luc Ollivier Merson, whose drawings from his paintings are very decorative in feeling. In Germany there is an endless number of draughtsmen who use the work of Dürer to a greater or less degree, copying it without the least attempt to adapt it to the special subjects they are illustrating. But I cannot attempt to give a complete list of the decorators for the simple reason that all illustrators are decorators.

Decoration is appropriateness, and it really makes no difference whether it is realistic or conventional, so long as it improves the appearance of the page. But at the same time I consider the modern thoroughly developed realistic work in its best form superior to that of the old men, because it shows most plainly the advances we have made in knowledge and technique. However, I cannot conceive how any liberal-minded person can fail to appreciate the fine qualities contained in the two drawings of birds by Habert-Dys and Herbert

Horne, one done with all the feeling of the nineteenth century, the other, good as it is, but a copy of the sixteenth. Both are equally decorative.

Nowhere for a moment will such a statement be questioned, except in this country. But here, within the last thirty years, people have been continuously taught to believe that book decoration, like all other art work, to be artistic must have a spiritual, moral, social, political, literary, or sixteenth-century value, while beauty of line and perfection of execution have been subordinated to these qualities; as a result the many pay no attention to the real artistic merits or defects of a drawing, but simply consider it from an entirely inartistic standpoint. The excuse is the elevation of the masses and the reformation of the classes. Art will never accomplish either of these desirable ends, its only function being to give pleasure, but this pleasure will be obtained from good work produced in any fashion. If the work is equally well, or, as usually happens, better done in a modern style, it will give more pleasure to a greater number, simply because it will be far more widely understood.

MATERIALS FOR PEN DRAWING

MATERIALS FOR PEN DRAWING

AS I have said before, the making of a pen drawing is the simplest process possible. Only four things are absolutely necessary—that is besides the rather indispensable qualification, ability. First, a piece of white paper; second, a hard lead-pencil, with its adjuncts, a very sharp knife and a rubber; third, a pen; and fourth, a bottle of ink.

First, as to the paper: the photo-engraver will tell you that the only paper to be used is hard white Bristol board, which undoubtedly is excellent, and can be worked on more freely with less practice than any other paper. When I say with less practice, I mean you must have just about the same amount of preparation as a great violinist has before he ever appears in public. The comparison is not out of place, for there are not more great pen draughtsmen to-day than there are great violinists. But Bristol board is at times very cumbersome to take about with one; when it is more than two sheets in thickness it will not roll without breaking. Though I know every photo-engraver will declare that my advice will "drive him mad," I can recommend several other kinds of paper on which good results can be had. As to whose Bristol board you use, it is of no particular importance. Goodall's is excellent, but as good is made by Pierre and Sons, and other firms. I have heard that Reeves' mounting board is also good. You must only be careful to get a board which is uniformly hard, and has been well dried, and through the surface of which the pen will not cut as it does sometimes on badly made boards. With good Bristol board, a good pen and great practice, you ought to be able to draw as freely in any direction as with a needle on an etching plate. But you cannot do this after six weeks' or even six months' work. The chances are you will never be able to. It is interesting to know that Vierge uses Bristol board. You can see the trade mark, Bristol A. L., in a garter, a very well-known mark, shining through a drawing on page 73 of *Pablo de Ségovie*, a book which no one who cares about pen drawing should fail to possess.

Probably the next easiest paper to draw on with a pen is London board, which I believe is Whatman paper pressed into sheets. It is usually very good, but you must be very careful to get it from a reliable dealer, or you will be sure to find soft places. I have always had mine from Newman in Soho Square and have found it excellent. However, any thin smooth paper, mounted and pressed, is extremely good, and if you go to Roberson and Co., Long Acre, they will mount and press it for you better than any one I know of.

The next paper I might mention is one against which I know photo-engravers will and do exclaim, that is good, hard, smooth writing-paper without any lines or water marks. Why they object I do not know, as either they or the artist, after the drawing has been made, can with a little care mount the paper, thus making it as solid as Bristol board. The results are certainly equal to those to be obtained on Bristol board. I have made many drawings on this paper. More-over, a great convenience is that in making a tracing from an original sketch in which you may wish to preserve its fresh feeling, you can fasten a sheet of thin hard correspondence paper over your original sketch, and the paper being so thin, you can see the drawing right through and work on the top of it. Lalanne and many others used paper of this kind.

Another paper is good hard Whatman paper with a slight grain. The photo-engraver will object to this too, but in the reproduction the result is a broken line, which, in the case of old houses, gives a richness to be had in no other way. This is a point on which most writers on art would give very explicit and elaborate directions. But all I shall say is, if you use Whatman paper, get whatever kind or quality suits you best. It is all very hard to work on at first, because the pen catches in the interstices of the grain, splutters and drags over the paper, and often runs into it, making a great blot very difficult to erase. I find Newman's art tablets, which consist of Whatman paper pasted on both sides of a stiff board, excellent. You can work on both sides and then split the tablet down the middle. It may be well to note that to remove blots, or to tone down lines that are too hard, a very useful instrument is a razor; though there is a French eraser with a curved blade, made for working on *Papier Gillot*, which is still better. The simplest plan, however, is to paste a piece of paper over the blot, and to join the lines at the edges.

White crayon papers are used most cleverly by Frenchmen, like Ulysse Butin and Lhermitte, and by Americans, especially by Tabor and Lungren; while Reinhart works on Bristol board in the same way. Part of the drawing, which is usually large and bold, is put in with ordinary lithographic crayon, or *crayon conté*, some of the blacks often with a brush, and the delicate work with a pen. The grain, or crayon, leaves ridges, which of course reproduce white. No attempt must be made to use stumps, or to get an even tone by filling up these accidental whites. The result is like a charcoal drawing with pen work on it.

There are various sorts of grained paper, the most popular being that with a horizontal line, which may be taken for the middle tone, as on a grey toned paper; on scratching this with a sharp knife either before or after you have drawn on it, a vertical line in white appears under, doubling the lightness of the light tone; this may be again scratched into pure white. There are three difficulties in using this paper. One is that the effect of these accurately drawn lines in the paper is always more or less mechanical; another, that the drawing cannot be reduced in size very much without blurring and indistinctness; and the third is that there is a great tendency to blots. This paper has been most successfully managed by Vierge, some of whose drawings made on it, and reproduced in *Le Monde Illustré*, are, like all his other work, the wonder and despair of every artist. Adrien Marie and Montalti have also used it very cleverly, and on it Adolf Ringel can perfectly reproduce his own bronzes. I have tried enough just to know how difficult and unsatisfactory the paper is. It is to be had from almost all the French photo-engraving houses in Paris, and from the colour shop at the foot of Regent Street. There are numerous varieties; some have dots, some lines, and some chalky surfaces on which you draw, or try to draw, and then lighten your drawing by scratching through it. You can also wash with colour and scratch through it. Sandham in America uses this paper to a very great extent. Personally I do not care for drawings made on it, with the exception of those of Vierge, who seems to have succeeded perfectly with it as with everything else he puts his hand to. Some of the drawings in *Pablo de Ségovie* seem to have been made on paper of this kind, though the white lines may have been cut through by the engraver, but of this I shall speak later. However, such draughtsmen as Rico and Abbey use ordinary white paper.

Of the second necessary, a hard lead-pencil, all I shall say is that you will want it, as well as a rubber; why, I shall explain farther on.

With the pen as with the paper, it is a case of finding out what suits you, and then using it. But I do not think the photo-engraver will object to any sort of pen. Half a dozen different kinds are often useful in the same drawing. The most useful all-round pen I know of is Gillott's Lithographic Crow Quill, No. 659, which, when once you have mastered it, can be used with the utmost freedom for any-thing, from the boldest to the most delicate line. It is almost like a living thing; it springs and responds to every impulse of your hand, and is vastly more pleasant than the dull heavy etching needle. There are many other crow quill pens, but they are all cheap, and, my experience is, very nasty. A J pen is very useful at times. In fact any pen you like is serviceable, and what you ought to use. An ordinary sharp school pen is as good as anything you can have. A quill pen works beautifully on Whatman paper in any direction, no matter how you hold it, and you can almost wash with the back of it, using it as a brush. Vierge, who has used everything, and men who have made pen and ink copies of Corot's pictures in order to get something of their softness, have used a double lined pen, but of this I have had no practical experience. Sometimes a quill pen will wear so that you can make this double line with it. The author of the *Excellency of the Pen and Pencil*, published in 1668, recommends "pens made of a raven's quill, which will strike a more neat stroke than the common quill," but for the truth of this I cannot answer. I have endeavoured to use various sorts of stylographic and fountain pens, which theoretically are perfect. But I have found that, unless charged with a very watery writing fluid which is sold with them, but would not answer for reproductive pen drawing, they are practically useless. It is a pity that makers cannot produce a fountain pen which an artist could use.

Only lately, in trying to find out what ink a certain pen draughtsman used, I was told it was a profound secret. And yet by the aid of a photo-engraver and the careful analysis of a corner of one of his drawings, in fifteen minutes there was no great difficulty in discovering that it was Winsor and Newton's liquid lamp black, which is sold at sixpence or a shilling a bottle. Of such stuff are made most of the secrets of art. To know what good ink is, and then to get it, means ease in drawing and success in reproduction. I suppose in this regard I am in the same condition as all other pen draughtsmen, each of whom thinks he has the best ink. I might as well give at once the name of the ink I use, and which of course I believe cannot be equalled. It is Higgins's American Drawing Ink, not to be bought at present in England. But it can be had by sending to G. S. Woolman, 116 Fulton Street, New York. The price for which an artist can get it from any dealer in artists' materials in America is twenty-five cents, or a shilling a bottle. Woolman, however, will charge, or endeavour to, about sixpence a bottle more, and the expressage from New York to London, which makes it cost about a guinea a dozen. It is therefore not cheap, but it is well worth the price. There is no ink equal to it for half a dozen reasons. First, it is put in a sensible flat bottle almost impossible to upset. It has a cork with a quill running through it which forms a handle, and thus keeps your fingers clean, prevents the cork from dropping into the bottle, keeps the ink off anything on which you may lay the cork, so beautifully is it balanced, while there is a pen-wiper attached. I know of no other ink for artists which is put up in so sensible a manner. Every one who draws knows how much ink usually goes on one's clothes and surroundings. As the quill in the cork reaches to the very bottom of the bottle, every time you pull it out, you stir the ink, so that there is no necessity to shake up the bottle, and the ink over yourself, as so frequently happens. Another advantage is that the bottle is filled with ink, and not with dirty water and a solid sediment which settles at the bottom, if it is left alone for half an hour. This ink is just as good at the last drop as when you open the bottle. I never knew but one photo-engraver to complain of it. It is jet black without shine, flows freely, and never clogs the pen. In short, from the time you open the bottle until you have put all its contents on paper, you have no reason to find fault with it. It is made in two qualities, water proof and not water proof.

Encre de Chine Liquide is very good, but I do not think it equals Higgins's ink. Liquid lamp black is a dead black and has no shine, and therefore reproduces well. Windsor and Newton's, Newman's,[1] and in fact all made artists' inks I have tried, have this fault : the ink sinks to the bottom of the bottle, leaving a dirty grey liquid. The makers will tell you that an advantage of their ink is that it will wash ; but what the artist wants primarily is to make, not a wash, but a black and white pen and ink drawing. Of course, theoretically, India ink is excellent. But it not only shines, which is unsuitable for photo-engraving, but it is very tedious to grind it down for yourself, and almost impossible to keep it a uniform black. Almost all the preparations I know of are abominable. Brown inks are very pretty to look at, but of course are utterly worthless for reproduction, because the delicate brown tone is all lost, and your drawing is nearly always printed in black, not in brown.

I do not think there is any other recommendation to be made, except to insist on the fact that good materials must be used if good results are wanted. But enough materials to make several pen drawings can be had for half a crown.

[1] Mr. Mills of Newman's has been, at my suggestion, making many experiments. Their ink is now very much better.

TECHNICAL SUGGESTIONS FOR
PEN DRAWING

TECHNICAL SUGGESTIONS FOR
PEN DRAWING

M OST writers on any branch of art begin by laying down definite laws for working. Mr. Hamerton in his *Etching and Etchers* says that the great value in an etching depends upon the etcher's own individuality in his method of work. He then goes on to give, in the most clear and lucid manner, directions for making an etching. I have faithfully followed Mr. Hamerton's suggestions, and I know into what quagmires they have led me; not from any fault of his, but simply because his methods were not suited to my needs. I therefore know by experience that a man must work in his own way; that what is good for one is simply artistic death for another.

One of the truest old artistic saws is that art can be learned but not taught. Therefore I do not intend to give infallible laws or directions on the subject of pen drawing, I only wish to make suggestions which are the result of a considerable amount of experience. But the study of good work is really of more practical value to the student than suggestions, and to show a series of examples of the best is the reason for the publication of this book.

Theoretically, it is very easy to take a piece of white paper, a pen, and any kind of ink, and draw away. This is really what the old men did, not minding blots or anything else, so long as they suggested the idea at which they aimed, and very charming are many of the sketches they produced in this manner. But now, pen and ink drawing is another thing.

I might start by saying, though it sounds as if I were trying to make a bull, that the best way to make a pen drawing is to make a pencil drawing. Whoever can make a good pen drawing without a preliminary pencil sketch of more or less importance, may set himself up for a genius, and be congratulated on his ability to avoid much drudgery. For convenience sake it will be better to suppose that my readers are not geniuses, and after all I shall only be ranking them temporarily with men like Fortuny and Rico. I know a study by Fortuny of a man draped, in which may be seen under the drawing, not only the nude figure, but the anatomy as well, drawn in pencil which has never been rubbed out. I have seen Rico on the canals of Venice making a pencil drawing more elaborate than the work which was to succeed it. In *L'Art*, vol. i., 1884, p. 63, there is an unfinished pen drawing by Louis Leloir, which is the strongest proof of what I say on this subject. One side is worked out with pen, the other is in the preliminary pencil. The pencil has all the care and reverence of a hard-working but brilliant student, and the pen, the freedom of an accomplished master, who knows he has a good foundation and goes ahead. Ruskin tells the student to make outlines with a hard pencil, and also that a drawing should be, not only free but right. Other men, Blum and Brennan, I have been told, never make a preliminary pencil sketch. It is to be hoped the reader is, but to be feared he is not, as clever as they are.

The best way is to make a careful sketch with a hard, an H, or HH lead-pencil on the sheet of paper on which you intend to make your pen drawing, in which case, in order to save the surface of the paper, only outline your shadows. In fact, make the sketch in outline as much as possible, as it must be rubbed out afterwards, and much rubbing will spoil the surface and grey the ink. Or make the drawing just as you want it on another sheet of paper, and then transfer it by means of black transferring paper, or else, as I suggested, use thin correspondence paper. When this is done, go to work with your pen.   It would be well to study from masters of pen drawing, but you must remember, if you study from reproductions, to choose only masterpieces, and that these, unless they are the same size, do not look like the original drawings, and even if they are the same size, much delicacy, refinement, and greyness of line have been lost.   In this book several of the most important drawings are reproduced by photogravure exactly the size they were made, and can therefore be followed line for line.   As a rule, however, the drawings are very much reduced, and you are consequently not looking at the drawing as it was made, but at the reproduction the artist wanted you to see.   Therefore it must be borne in mind that the artist made his drawing, not necessarily crude, but with the lines farther apart than you see them, because, if these drawings have to be reduced very much, the spaces between the lines are so diminished that, unless the printing is very careful, as in the best American magazines and books, you have, instead of the delicate grey drawing you expected, a dirty black mass, owing to the ink filling up the spaces between the lines and to the lines themselves running together.

I hope it will be understood that this is not a manual for beginners, and that I am not concerned with such questions as, " How do you draw trees?" or, " How do you make bricks?"   You go to nature and draw them as faithfully as you would if you were drawing with a pencil or painting in oils.   As to light and shade, colour and tone, pen drawing is subject to the same laws as crayon drawing, pencil drawing, and etching.   There is, therefore, no necessity for my going into detail on the subject.

You must remember that if you want a sharp line, your work must be perfectly black, and must stand out clean and alone on the paper.   If you want to get a grey, you will not succeed by putting water in the ink, but by making the lines light—I mean fine and separate.   This is the general rule to follow.   Of course a master will grey his lines, and run them together, and make a tender grey where the student would make but a muddle, and in fact do all sorts of things that I might say should not be done.   You will also find that if you put one solitary line in the sky to mark the outline of a cloud, it will come out in the reproduction three times as strong as you intended it to, for the simple reason that though four or five light grey

lines may stand up together, one will not, and will have to be thickened
in the type-metal by the photo-engraver.   Of course in a photogravure
you can get the lines as fine as you choose to make them.   In
drawing your foreground, do not make it too coarse under the
impression that it will be brought by reproduction into proper
relations with the delicate distance.   It probably will always remain
coarse.   Though there are few things to be remembered in connection
with pen drawing, these few that I have mentioned, such as keeping
the lines apart, not getting too many blacks, are of the utmost
importance.   But these are things which must be remembered in
any sort of drawing, if you want a good result.

The size of pen drawings for reproduction is a matter of experience and personal liking.   It is not, as the photo-engraver insists,
necessary to make the drawing one-third or one-half as wide again
as the block is to be.   Of course if your drawing is to fill exactly a
certain space, you will have to shape it to fit in.   But in most
magazines or books the space is made to suit the drawing, and
all the art editor need do is to reduce the longest side of the
drawing to fit his page, and the type will come in around it.   As
to size, for example I believe in many cases Mr. Parsons' drawings
are exactly the same, or very slightly larger than their reproductions,
a contradiction—also proven in this book—to the photo-engraver's
oft-repeated statement that drawings must be reduced in order to
get fine work.   On the other hand, I have frequently seen drawings
by Brennan which filled a sheet of Whatman imperial paper, and
were reduced—and beautifully—to five inches the longest way.   But
for general advice, it would probably be wisest for the draughtsman
to make his drawing twice the width of the intended reproduction.

There are many devices adopted by every clever pen draughtsman,
which to the purist are very shocking.   As, for example, in putting
on in two minutes a flat tone with a brush, which will afterwards
be rouletted by the photo-engraver.   It is really a question of getting
what is wanted in five minutes or in five hours.   Often, too, one
finds that the distance comes entirely too strong, and will have to
be toned down by a skilful engraver.   Frequently the engravings
of French drawings will be cut all over in this way, and are thus
given a soft grey misty effect, often very beautiful.   Nearly all the
better pen drawings in *Harper's* and the *Century* are hand-worked,

as it is called, by skilful engravers. All fine work must be cut at the edges if you do not want it to look hard and rough.

The thumb is a very useful auxiliary in pen drawing. By inking your thumb, and pressing it on the paper, you can often get a strong rich effect, the lines on the skin being marked on the paper, and reproducing beautifully.

In Fortuny's work are to be found dear delightfully-smeared dirty blotches, a trial to the purist, but a joy to the artist, since their value and expression are always just right.

A foreground, old walls of houses, can be richly varied very beautifully by taking a tooth brush, dipping it in ink, and then running a match stick under it, and splattering the necessary parts of the drawing, stopping the others out with paper. The most charming effects are to be had in this way. But any one who goes into pen drawing, will learn all these and more devices in a very short time if he has any facility for it. But he will also learn that pen drawing is an art which requires as much skill and experience on the part of the artist as etching does, and though less treacherous, and much more simple in its actual mechanical operation, is also much less dependent on accidental effects than etching. But the great thing to remember is, not to try to draw everything under the sun with a pen, but only those things which by simplification lend themselves easily and naturally to it. I have already said, you must know how to draw before you can make a pen drawing, and after you have learned to draw, you must be able to arrange the most simple lines in the most artistic manner, or else you will never be a great pen draughtsman. It is just this want of artistic feeling for line that makes a man, who may be a great painter, say "O scribble it down anyway," with a bad drawing as the result. While if you take a pen drawing by a great master you will find that, though it may look as if it was scribbled down hurriedly and hastily, it is done with the greatest care.

I hope none of my readers would be so foolish as to follow the calmly-given advice of Mr. H. R. Robertson, to copy woodcuts or steel engravings of any subjects except those done with the pen, and never then if you can help it. As Mr. Hamerton says: "There is a wide distinction in every art between possibility and prudence. A delicate line engraving *may* be so closely imitated with a fine pen that few people, at a little distance, would at the first glance detect the difference; but no artist who knew the value of his time would waste it in such foolish toil." The only sensible course, if you must copy, is to copy pen drawings of the greatest pen draughtsmen, if you can see the originals; if you can only see their reproductions, to remember that these have been reduced. For a man to say that pen drawings are obtained in two distinct methods, one by a few lines drawn slowly, the other by many lines drawn rapidly, and then to cite Rembrandt as a man to be studied for the second method, is to suppose that everybody is an embryo Rembrandt. Had photo-engraving been invented when Mr. Ruskin wrote his *Elements of Drawing*, he never would have made the mistake of advising the draughtsman to cover quickly a space of paper with lines, without troubling himself as to how they are made, and then to place other sets of lines on top of them. Certainly the man who can with one set of lines get the exact grey, which according to Mr. Ruskin is to be produced with many sets, will be not only doing a much more artistic piece of work, but saving much time. The consequence is, if one wishes to get a grey he should cover his paper with straightish lines, troubling himself infinitely to draw them very carefully.

As a matter of fact, what you want to do is to take the French advice and, no matter how good a draughtsman you may be, go slowly at first in order that you may go fast in the end.

REPRODUCTION OF PEN DRAWINGS

REPRODUCTION OF PEN DRAWINGS

PEN drawings may be reproduced in two radically different ways. First, by what is commonly known among artists as photo-engraving or process, for printing with the type in book, magazine, or newspaper; and secondly, by photogravure on a copper or other plate, for printing like a steel plate or etching. These two processes may be subdivided, the first into innumerable methods, and the second into a dozen or more. In the first, the object is to make a relief block, as I have said, for printing with type; and in the second, to produce an engraved plate for printing separately. Examples of both are given throughout the book.

In the photo-engraving, the drawing is photographed and then directly etched into a zinc plate, or, after numerous processes, finds itself on a gelatine or some other film, the film in relief with the drawing sunken in it. From this film a casting is made, from which electros may be taken in relief just exactly like type. The production of this result would be neither clear nor interesting to any but a photo-engraver or a photographer. It would require a whole book to be explained, as it has been, and very well, in *Modern Methods of Book Illustration*.

Photogravures are similarly produced by photographing the drawing on to a copper plate, which is then bitten more or less in the same manner as an etching, and worked up afterwards with a graver, or by building up a plate in a bath on a gelatinous film.   The result resembles an etching closely.

Reproduction is a purely mechanical process, but so important as to be destined almost entirely to supersede all but the best wood-engraving, and all other sorts of reproductive art.   In it no human intelligence comes between the drawing and the result to any great degree, although intelligent aid can always be given.   For example, it is almost impossible for a wood-engraver to cut the delicate grey lines of many a pen drawing.   It is equally impossible for the photo-engraver to reproduce them mechanically.   But their intelligent co-operation, added to the accuracy of the process, will give the desired effect.   I mean the fine line which the wood-engraver cannot cut by himself, and which is so fine that if reproduced accurately it will scarcely stand on the process block, can be cut down to the required fineness on the relief block by the wood-engraver, or by the photo-engraver, if he is artist enough to do it.

Mr. Hamerton sets forth the great economy of process reproductions as one of their chief advantages.   " It so happens," he writes, " that nothing we can draw reproduces quite so perfectly as a clear black ink line on perfectly smooth white paper, and in consequence of this the art of drawing with the pen has suddenly become the principal means of disseminating artistic ideas when economy is an object."   But it is very doubtful whether a cheap photo-engraving is really much cheaper than a cheap woodcut.   The latter will look better, as it is almost impossible to print a cheap process block.   Publishers should reject all but the best reproductions by photographic processes.   Otherwise they only lead to carelessness and the ruin of the artist's drawing.

Of course it would do the pen draughtsman no harm, but rather an enormous amount of good, to not only study with the photo-engraver before he sets himself up as a draughtsman, but also whenever his work is being reproduced.   No explanation will supply the criticisms which an intelligent photo-engraver will make on a novice's drawings, that is criticising them with a view to their reproduction.   Unless men to-day are willing to come out of their luxurious studios— as some of the best do—and go down to the dirty shop of the photo-engraver and try experiments, or intelligently consult with him, we shall never have really artistic workmen and thoroughly good results.

There are certain processes by which results resembling pen drawings are produced. Prepared surfaces of paraffin, or other materials from which a cast can be made, are laid on plates of blackened brass or other metal, and you draw with a sharp point through the film of paraffin, and a cast is taken from the drawing so made. The result is very like a sharp pen drawing. But there are two great difficulties to be surmounted; one is that reduction is impossible, and the drawing must therefore be the size of the desired print, and the other is that the mechanical process is much harder to learn than drawing with a pen, and entirely different. The technical difficulties are really so great as to be scarcely worth the trouble of overcoming. They have been mastered, however, with some very good results by Herkomer and Dawson, the inventor. Randolph Caldecott also tried this process; and the late Kent Thomas did some extraordinary things with it. I believe it is excellent for the drawing of maps.

Since the introduction of photo-lithography, it has not been necessary for an artist who is a draughtsman to become a skilled lithographer in order to have his line drawings reproduced on stone. For though he should understand the process, there is no more reason why he should give his time to it than that he should reproduce his own drawings by photo-engraving. Intelligent supervision of reproduction is one thing; unintelligent waste of time over mechanical details is quite another. The drawing of the Ponce de Leon Hotel by Blum, and the example of Waldemar Frederick in the German Chapter, have been reproduced by some form of lithographic process.

The real advantage of mechanical reproduction can be easily explained. Unless the artist draws expressly with the thought of the woodcutting of every single line he is making, no wood-engraver can follow him. It will be said that the draughtsmen on wood of Dürer's time did this; but it really is not likely that they often did. So tedious, so difficult, and so laborious is this manner of working that, not only is it an exploded theory that Dürer cut his own blocks, but I believe he scarcely ever even drew on the wood. It is more probable that he made the studies which we possess to-day, that these studies were traced or enlarged or reduced on to the block by his pupils, or by the woodcutter himself, that the design was then touched up by Dürer and cut by the engraver. It is impossible otherwise that he could have produced such an amount of work. I say this as a practical illustrator, knowing perfectly well the time which must have been given to one of these drawings. Besides, this was the course the old men always adopted in their other art work; they had a shop full of clever young students, whose hands and brains they used whenever they could. If Dürer, the typical illustrator at any rate of the Middle Ages, drew every line for the woodcutter with a handling utterly different from that which we see in all his etchings, the lesser men who surrounded and followed him and would have been influenced by him, did nothing of the sort. They made their drawings on the block with the greatest care, in inks of different degrees of blackness, and with beautifully arranged lines, and the wood-engraver cut the blocks without the slightest feeling for the artist's work. It might very reasonably be asked why did I not then use more of the old drawings? Because, made on the wood-blocks, they were cut all to pieces, the engravers not following the artist's lines, but engraving lines which were easy to cut, ignoring all but the main ideas of the design, and being, I maintain, incapable, slovenly, or slipshod, and not to be compared for a minute to the engravers who have been developed since the time of Menzel. When they did follow the original lines, it was only because the artist drew expressly for them, as did the English draughtsmen of thirty years ago. Everything I say can be proven by a reference to the spoiled wood-blocks, the only evidence we have, but all we need, in the Plantin Museum. These drawings were made on the block in exactly the same way as the draughtsman works on paper to-day. But I have not used them for two reasons: they could not be reproduced without infinite labour, since they are spoiled blocks, and, having been made three hundred years ago, are faded; and, moreover, they are no better than work done to-day.

It may be objected that I have elsewhere stated one must draw specially for reproduction. But the requirements in this case are even at the present moment the simplest, and may be done away with in the future; nothing is necessary but a reasonably clean line, good ink and white paper. The reason that a certain number of examples throughout the book are cut on wood is not that process was unable to reproduce them, but either that the engravings were made before the time of process or that the artists were too indifferent as to the quality of their ink or paper. There is not a single wood-cut in the book from which a process block could not be made so cleverly that it would be impossible to tell, were they placed side by side, which was the original block and which the process. The photo-engraving, however, is really superior to the wood-engraving for this reason: there are not a dozen engravers who can equal the best process. The work of J. D. Cooper, Paterson, and Swain I have shown; that of Whitney, Cole, and Collins can be seen in almost any number of the *Century*. Cole's marvellous reproduction of the head of Lincoln after a drawing by Wyatt Eaton in the Scribner collection of proofs from that magazine, now the *Century*, should be mentioned in this connection; and I now give a woodcut by the Frenchman, Charles Beaude. These men, and probably a few others, are the only engravers who can equal process. Some of Cooper's work is as good as any process. Cole's Lincoln gives Wyatt Eaton's drawing because it was drawn for him. But the portrait by Wyatt Eaton reproduced by process in the American Chapter is far more freely drawn, and there is no wood-engraving about it. The cut by Beaude after Edelfeldt is most remarkable. Any woodcutter can show the actual lines, this being the easiest thing possible to do, so long as there is not too much fine cross-hatching in the drawing. But few can give the pen quality of the line, which is extremely difficult. The men to whom I have referred can. So, too, could some of Menzel's engravers and some of the English engravers of thirty years ago, though none ever surpassed the work of Beaude. But the minute even Beaude comes to the elaborate cross-hatching, the delicate greys, or the pencil marks in the drawing, he meets an insurmountable barrier. I say most un-hesitatingly that marvellous as is his woodcut, I much prefer to it the process blocks after Louis Leloir and Lalauze in the French Chapter.

But suppose that none of this cross-hatching, these delicate greys or pencil marks existed in the drawing, and that the wood-engraver could cut a perfect facsimile in line and in feeling; it is a crying shame to put an artist of such consummate ability to doing the work a machine can accomplish equally well in as many hours as he would take days. There is no more false subjection of art to mechanism in the adoption of process than there was in the substitution of movable types for block types, in the development of woodcutting in the time of Dürer, in the resurrection made by Bewick, in the famous white line loved by Mr. Linton, in the use of the steam press, or in any other development. Why, if we had not made use of these improvements and hundreds of others, we would not even have been

apes and winkles! The minute that any real and true improvement is introduced and shown to be an improvement, we are blind and fools not to adopt it. It is not its cheapness which gives value to process; neither is it the inability of woodcutting to obtain the same results—a great engraver almost can; but it is the fact that unless this great artist wishes to display his power, it is useless to compel a wood-engraver—a vastly different person from a woodcutter —to toil and slave for a result in which a machine so often surpasses him. In a word, this book is merely an exhibition of the best possible pen drawings I could obtain and the best possible mechanical reproductions of them. It is a plea for pen drawing and an exposition of process.

These three prints of Dürer's Big Horse will show the difference in the three methods of reproducing the same engraving better than any amount of written explanation. The first example is a woodcut by Paterson. A careful comparison of it with the photo-engraving by the Dawsons, entirely a mechanical reproduction, on the following page, will make clear the points wherein the photo-engraving fails and the wood-engraver has succeeded. But the failures of the mechanical photo-engraving have been less than those of the skilled craftsman, and the results obtained by photography are truer than those obtained by the wood-engraver; the block mechanically reproduced under the supervision of Alfred Dawson, without any hand-work on it at all, has much more of the feeling of Dürer's work than Paterson's engraving. The reason for this is simple. The lines are directly and automatically reproduced by photography, while each one has to be re-made by the wood-engraver. The photo-engraver has reproduced the actual lines of Dürer; the wood-engraver has had to cut around and produce new ones for himself, which never can be perfectly done. The Dawsons' block contains no more lines than Paterson's engraving,—in fact it does not contain as many, for Paterson has added some that do not exist in the original, and patched up certain imperfections in the original plate, giving in consequence a certain wooden feeling to his block and not the look of metal lines, but this the Dawsons have reproduced in their block, which therefore comes nearer to the original engraving. Of course the photogravure is still truer to the original because it contains the tone of ink and colour of time found on the print in the British Museum, and shows that fulness of colour which no wood or process engraving has yet been able to obtain. These differences between the woodcut and the process block can only be appreciated by students, though they should be by collectors. To feel them, a long study of the cuts will be necessary, and an examination of the blocks and a comparison with the original is the only way in which they can be appreciated. The reproduction of a line engraving by woodcutting is one of the most difficult operations possible;

the reproduction of a line engraving by photo-engraving is really absurdly easy.

As to the photogravure also made by the Dawsons, it is not nearly so much better than their photo-engraved block as it should

be. It ought to be a perfect facsimile, but though it is probably as good as anything that could be done in England, it does not compare with the plate of the same subject by Amand-Durand, which, owing to an unfortunate business complication, I could not use. To have properly shown the absolute difference between these forms of re-

production and the original, as well as the manner in which they vary from it, I should have given prints from the Dürer plate. This being impossible, I have tried to point out how they differ from each other. But even though I have explained that both of

the plates by the Dawsons are mechanically reproduced, as in fact are all the photogravures in the book, I have no doubt that many people will speak of them as etchings and call the process blocks woodcuts. This wilful ignorance on the part of critics and the public would do no special harm, if it were not that certain publishers

are taking advantage of it at the present time to palm off mechanically reproduced plates as etchings, attaching a fictitious value to
them, thus perpetrating a fraud. A careful study of the different
quality of line and the different points in which the three plates
fail and succeed, is the only way in which one can distinguish
between an etching and a photogravure, a process block and a
woodcut.

In all my references to old work, I have used the name of Dürer,
but I do not mean to imply that Dürer was the only illustrator in
the past. I could have proved what I wished as well by reference
to other artists or engravers on steel or wood or copper—to the work
of Lucas Van Leyden, Mantegna, Martin Schongaur, Lucas Cranach,
Hans Holbein, the Venetians, Botticelli, or even Claude. But just
as Adolf Menzel in Germany is the embodiment of modern pen
drawing, in fact of modern illustration, so is Albert Dürer of illustration in the past. The motives of other days have been given up;
the motives of to-day have replaced them. Which are the greater
and which the lesser, I have no intention of discussing. As to
technique, of far more importance, it is now infinitely better, and I
do not hesitate to maintain that if Dürer were alive to-day, he would
do twice as good work as he ever did. For Dürer had to draw
directly for the engraver, and then he was not sure of getting the
results he wanted; the modern illustrator draws for himself.

Neither have I given another example of that oft trotted out
Egyptian brick stamp, nor turned up as a trump the everlasting
playing card, nor quarrelled over the original Saint Christopher.
Indeed, I have purposely omitted all this old work, and begun
where the usual authority leaves off. For I hold that if writers
would only pay some slight attention to what is going on around
them, and stop disputing over the unknowable and undiscoverable
in the past, they would at least collect data which would serve as a
basis for historians of art in the future. Pen drawing or illustration,
the art of to-day, has so far been quite as much ignored as wood-
engraving was in its early stages of development. The illustrators of
the Middle Ages worked for the people; so do the illustrators of
to-day.

HOPES AND FEARS FOR PEN DRAWING

HOPES AND FEARS FOR PEN DRAWING

I HAVE tried to show what pen drawing is, and in conclusion I should like to state my great hopes, and greater fears, for the future of the art. I have already pointed out that pen drawing is supposed to be despised by almost everybody but a few artists and art editors, some of the latter having given it recognition simply because of its cheapness for reproduction. I hope therefore to see an art, which is looked down upon to-day by the same people who despised etching until Mr. Hamerton opened their eyes to its true value, put in its proper place—that is, in equal rank with etching.

A good etching is only a successful pen drawing after all. The qualities of softness, richness, and mistiness can be given by a master of pen drawing, and reproduced in photogravure so cleverly, as to deceive the most accomplished art critic. Smudges, accidental foul biting, and a thousand other things that go to make the value of the state of an etching by Whistler, Haden, or Méryon, can be obtained in ten minutes by a clever man with an old tooth brush and a rough skinned thumb, while the drawing, the only autographic and valuable part of the production, is exactly the same, and the tone, the softness, and effect of any unwiped plate can be produced by a good printer for a few pence extra. It is really for blemishes and defects, accidental or intentional on the part of the very thoughtful artist, that the collector prizes its rare first state. The value attached to the print from an etched plate is fictitious; the value of a pen drawing is real. The pen drawing is the artist's work; the etching is only a print from it, often not satisfactory to the artist, for though he sees just what he wants on the copper-plate, neither he nor the printer can get it from the plate to the paper. With the etching, as with the pen drawing, there is only one person who can own the original. A print from a photogravure of a pen drawing is really of as much value as the print from an etching. The only difference is that in nine cases out of ten the etching is a failure, the photogravure a success. The collector may own the single pen drawing, but he hardly ever troubles himself to buy the original copper-plate which is owned by the dealer, and which—and not the print from it—is the real equivalent to the pen drawing.[1] But so ignorant are some amateurs and collectors that they pay high prices for artists' proofs of photogravures and autotypes, which cannot even boast of rarity, and are only better than prints inasmuch as an early pull of any plate is of course sharper and clearer, and therefore better than a later one. I have heard the intelligent collector persuaded into paying £20 for an etching which was quite without artistic merit, and which in a few years will sell for 20s.; while, for a guinea or so more, he had a gorgeous frame thrown in, which, he was assured, he only got at that price because all the other subscribers were having exactly the same thing!

To value a work of art only for its rarity is a feeling with which I have no sympathy. But it is strange that collectors should not see that an original drawing which they can own and preserve, and which need not be duplicated if they do not wish it, is of more value according to their own standard than a print, which five hundred or fifty thousand other people can own, and over which they have no control. They are in fact influenced by dealers who publish almost all the etchings, and are not willing to encourage the work which would bring them comparatively small profit.

In a recent conversation with a dealer, he admitted my facts to be

---

[1] Of course the pecuniary value of a work of art is, like that of other things, determined by the law of supply and demand; but apart from this, the mere ambition to own a thing because no one else can duplicate it is, as Mr. Will H. Low says, "essentially vulgar, and when exercised in the domain of art excessively so." But then Mr. Low is an artist and not a collector.

perfectly true, but in the next breath he said he would fight against them so long as he continued in the print business. For the simple reason that he could purchase an etched plate for the same amount of money he would have to pay for a good pen drawing; that if the plate proved popular, he could sell thousands of proofs from it, some of which, containing cabalistic and inartistic scrawls, would bring ten times more than others which only contained the artist's signature, while these would sell for twice as much as the ordinary plain prints; the plain prints themselves being probably quite as good as the first pulls from the plate, because the artist now steels his plate the moment it is finished. Exactly the same result could be obtained by the dealer buying a pen drawing, having a photogravure made from it and selling the prints. I know that this result is to be had with absolute certainty, while every etching ordered by a dealer is an uncertain speculation. Still, if dealers would go to the leading pen draughtsmen of the day, they would be as sure to get good drawings as they are now certain of getting bad etchings from artless etchers. All that is needed is a little exploiting, but dealers will never do this for themselves. For all business—and etching is no longer an art, but only a business and a trade—is conducted on the most short-sighted principles—principles which are rapidly running etching into the ground. But until nothing more can be made from etchings, though the market is flooded with them, dealers will refuse to turn their attention to anything else. I know, as I have said, that if pen drawing can be made to seem worth the financial attention of dealers, the result will be, mainly, more money in their pockets. But still, with so many good pen draughtsmen now at work, it may show the public that there is at the present moment a healthy, flourishing art. However, somebody must compel the dealers to take up pen drawing, if it is to be taken up by them at all, for they will never do so of themselves.

The objection most art editors find to pen drawing is, that it is not understood by the masses. I have made many pen drawings, not only in the house, but among the people, and I have heard from them more expressions of pleasure in a pen drawing, both while it was being made and after it was finished, than I have ever heard given to a pencil or a wash drawing. The reason is easy to explain. In pen drawing the details, the windows of houses, the delicacy of trees or the study of a figure, half an inch high, are all worked out carefully, lovingly, and artistically, while in wash drawings these details may be only suggested, and to the average mortal artistic suggestion is absolutely meaningless.

That children like pen drawings needs no proof. The success of Randolph Caldecott's,[1] Kate Greenaway's, Adrien Marie's, and Reginald Birch's drawings,—whether they have a slight wash of colour or not is of no consequence,—answers all arguments to the contrary. Of course, as the educated child grows up, its innate ideas of art are so quickly suppressed that in the end bad drawings are not infrequently preferred to good. It is only wonderful that any one cares in the least for drawing.

That some people do, however, is proved by the popularity of magazines like the *Century* and *Harper's*, and of illustrated weeklies like *Le Monde Illustré*, and *Fliegende Blätter*. As far as I know, the utterly inartistic and pseudo-comic papers, which are usually illustrated by pen drawings, have the largest circulation of any illustrated English periodicals—*Ally Sloper's Half-Holiday*, for example, though I ought to add that, technically, the late Mr. Baxter's rendering of Ally Sloper was excessively clever.

Newspapers which really appeal to the masses, and in which there is never mention of the word art, are beginning to use pen drawings, some of which are not bad, though the majority are atrocious. A few of the portraits and little sketches that have appeared in the *Pall Mall Gazette* are good, but frequently they have been remarkable only for their artlessness. But it is in newspapers that my greatest hopes and fears for the future of pen drawing lie. I hope that some great inventor like Walter or Hoe [2] may turn his attention—as I believe he will—to artistic newspaper printing. If he does he will kill every magazine. For just as literary men are only too willing to work for the

---

[1] Some people say children do not appreciate Randolph Caldecott's work. But any one who was a child when his books began to come out, as I was, or who knows anything about children, need not be told that such a statement is not true.

[2] In fact, in a recent conversation with Mr. De Vinne of New York—the man who has done more to obtain the best results from artists' drawings than any one else, and whose work comes nearer satisfying artists than that of any other printer—he said he had been making experiments continuously for the last few years, in order that when there is a demand for good illustrated newspapers he will be able to print them.

newspapers, so would the pen draughtsman be, if he could get his work well printed. And this would merely mean bringing art to the people, where we are told it was in Italy some hundreds of years ago. For just as the people are said to have gone to church to see their art, so many now seek for everything, art included, in the newspapers. But I fear that when this comes to pass, the second state of art will be worse than the first, unless the newspaper office is revolutionised and an art editor introduced. For the news editor would very likely accept whatever came to hand.

Not only can an illustrated newspaper be printed daily, but more than one is published to-day. The New York *Daily Graphic* and the Paris *Charivari* are examples. The last time I saw the New York *Graphic*, however, it was still suffering under the disadvantage of not having any good men to work for it. Instead of employing good artists, it was content with cheap-looking work, just as the average newspaper, instead of getting a staff of men whose writing would give literary value to its columns, employs people whose special aim seems to be to write stupidly and to enlarge upon the power of journalism—*i.e.* of themselves. That their power is great, owing to the ignorance of the public, is unfortunately unquestionable. And for this reason, with the general use of drawings in papers, they would be able to bring art down to the same level to which they too frequently debase literature. In the illustrated daily of the future, the plan that will have to be pursued is this: all sorts of illustrated news must be reproduced by the Meisenbach or other process from photographs; slight sketches could be made by clever men in three or four hours, and reproduced in time to appear in the next, or possibly the same, day's paper; more important work must be delayed several days or a week, but still the daily would be much ahead of the weeklies with its news.

My greatest fear is only that such a paper would be an instant and phenomenal success, and that its managers would make their fortunes and then, like those of other papers started by a brilliant set of young artists, engravers, and journalists, become merely stock-holders, pocket the profits, and allow the paper to fall to a lower level than that of the publications it was going to improve. It is just this, one fears for pen drawing in every direction. The difficulty of keeping to a very high standard is shown in *L'Art*, which has very

noticeably gone down during the last few years. The only con-
solation is that pen drawing eventually ruins the people who use
it by abusing it. *Our Continent*, an American publication, which
started with the most brilliant prospects, was wrecked exactly from
this cause; it began to publish nothing but poor pen drawings
and quickly came to grief. Papers which do continue to improve
week by week and month by month are the *Century, Harper's,
Fliegende Blätter*. Unless there is an art editor who can draw to
himself a clever staff of artists and keep them, an illustrated paper
can neither go on, nor maintain the position it has reached.

There is an enormous demand for pen drawing growing daily,
and though the supply apparently equals it, pen drawing as an
art is not advancing. There are a few artists who really care
for it in itself, and endeavour with each new drawing to make
something of value, but outside of the larger magazines in which
their work usually appears, they apparently make no impression
on the majority of pen draughtsmen who are filling books and
papers with artless drawings. Any one who will look back,
especially through the European magazines and the *Century*, will
see that some of the very best pen drawings were made between
1879 and 1883, before this vast army of scribblers had sprung
up and found that their wretched work was of value to people as
ignorant as themselves. Just as architects are wanted to restore
or ruin whatever little beauty is left in the world, so this ever-
increasing army of pen draughtsmen, one might think, is wanted
to lower the standard of pen drawing and turn it farther and
farther away from its legitimate end.

Because so many pen drawings are now made, it has been
said that for artists who work in pen and ink "their only chance
of relative immortality is a reputation won in some other department
of art." A sufficient answer to this assertion is to be had in the
drawings of four men—to mention no more,—Fortuny, Rico, Menzel,
and Vierge, which will be known so long as there is any love
for art. It might as well be said that because thousands of artless
pictures are painted and exhibited every year, a good painter, in
order to be remembered, must make his reputation as a sculptor or an
architect.

Though it seems as if Mr. Hamerton and Mr. Haden have

shown people the beauty and true province of etching, only to make the fortune of print dealers and to set on pinnacles men who transgress every law governing etching as a fine art, yet at the same time, etchers like Whistler, Haden, and Buhot occasionally produce plates which prove the beauty and province of the art have not been entirely forgotten. In like manner there is a strong saving remnant among pen draughtsmen, and upon it hopes for the future of pen drawing can safely rest. But if good pen drawing is to be confined to these few men, and elsewhere to be used as a medium for disseminating the cheapest and worst art, the outlook is dark enough. Whether the few will leaven the whole is doubtful. But they certainly will never be swallowed up entirely, and their work, like all good art, will live.

INDEX

INDEX

PRINTERS · R & R · PAINTERS

EDINBURG·